Consociation and Voting
in Northern Ireland

National and Ethnic Conflict in the Twenty-First Century

Brendan O'Leary, Series Editor

Consociation and Voting in Northern Ireland

Party Competition and Electoral Behavior

John Garry

PENN

UNIVERSITY OF PENNSYLVANIA PRESS

PHILADELPHIA

Published by
University of Pennsylvania Press
Philadelphia, Pennsylvania 19104-4112
www.upenn.edu/pennpress

Printed in the United States of America on acid-free paper

10 9 8 7 6 5 4 3 2 1

Library of Congress Cataloging-in-Publication Data
ISBN 978-0-8122-4837-1

For my parents, John and Kathleen

Contents

Chapter 1

Consociation and Voting: Ideology, Performance, and Participation

What is the most appropriate institutional response to deep social division? This question, unsurprisingly, has long been the focus of attention of politicians and academics and has provoked heated debate in the policy and academic communities. One particular response to intense division is the implementation of consociational power-sharing institutions. This involves recognizing the distinct community or identity groups that are in conflict, facilitating the sharing of power between the rival groups in a highly inclusive coalition government, and providing each competing identity group with veto powers to protect their group interests.

A range of countries have been characterized as consociational, including Belgium, Lebanon, the Netherlands (1917–1967), Switzerland, Bosnia-Herzegovina, Macedonia, Burundi, and post-Apartheid South Africa. Proponents of consociation argue that the system is particularly valuable in terms of accommodating deep ethnic, language, or religious differences and providing the political stability and security in which democracy may flourish. In contrast, critics of consociational power sharing lament the implementation of what they see as elite-inspired undemocratic structures which cement rather than lessen the underlying potent (ethnic, language, or cultural) division. The arguments between proponents and opponents of consociational power sharing are directly relevant for the study of electoral democracy under consociational conditions.

From the critics' responses to supporters of consociation, it is possible to derive three sets of—observable—implications for party competition and citizens' electoral behavior.

First, critics argue that consociation heightens the salience of the underlying divide, and this leads to the continuance of distinct party systems, with one set of parties competing for votes from community A and a distinct set of parties competing for votes from community B; a process of "ethnic outbidding" whereby the extreme parties in each bloc become increasingly successful as public opinion polarizes; and the suffocation of any possible new dimensions of political competition. Second, critics imply that consociational democracy is a contradiction in terms, given that a highly inclusive power-sharing government undermines any role for "opposition" and prohibits voters from replacing a bad government with a different one. Thus, it is not possible for voters to hold the power-sharing government to account for its performance. Third, it is suggested that the elite nature of the consociational enterprise alienates ordinary citizens, who are likely to become further disengaged from politics and decline to participate at election time.

These criticisms may be seen to cast doubt on the normative desirability of consociation, portraying it as an institutional response that makes a bad situation worse and leads to a low quality of electoral democracy. It is not the primary aim of this book to engage in normative evaluation of the desirability or otherwise of consociation. It *is* the aim of this book to investigate whether the implications for electoral democracy of the critics' claims are empirically observable. The empirical investigation is conducted in one particular case of consociational government: the Northern Ireland 2007–2011 executive, which included all the main parties in the system and, dramatically and historically, brought together long-standing foes in a power-sharing government.

The next section of this chapter offers a description of the consociational response to deep division. I then clarify the specific consociational institutional arrangements operating in the Northern Ireland case. The main criticisms of consociation are then elaborated and the testable implications of these criticisms for citizen behavior at election time are specified.

The Consociational Response to Conflict

The consociational power-sharing response to conflict may be situated in a broad typology of possible institutional responses (O'Leary 2013). As illustrated in Figure 1.1, when faced with deep division in a place, one may respond with a simple insistence that people living in a given place should become as similar to each other as possible, or an equally simple insistence that it is perfectly acceptable for people to be very different from each other. On this continuum, ranging from a demand for homogeneity to a recognition of diversity, one may situate four responses to conflict. Closest to the demand for homogeneity are assimilationists, whose preference is for minorities who are "different" to blend into, and become more like, existing society. The minority culture is expected to adopt, or fuse with, the culture of the dominant majority. Difference is downplayed, there ought to be no distinct "minorities," and a single inclusive civic citizenship in a single society is emphasized. Accordingly, assimilationists favor majoritarian democratic institutions.

Slightly less demanding of homogeneity are integrationists, who draw a distinction between the acceptability of cultural differences in the public and private spheres. In the latter sphere, distinct cultural minorities may happily be allowed and expected to flourish, but in the former sphere they are not. In public space, minorities must leave their cultural identities

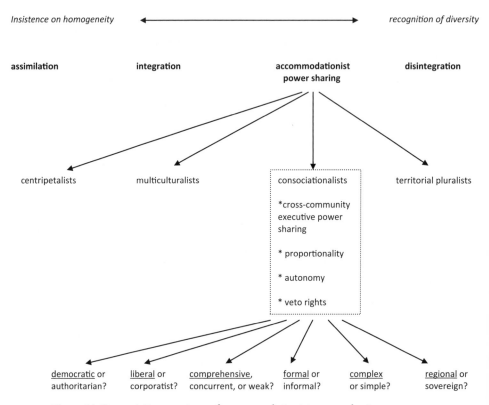

Figure 1.1. Consociation as a type of accommodationist power-sharing response to division (derived from O'Leary 2013).

behind; public institutions should be inclusive and, as far as possible, culturally neutral. Again, majoritarian institutions are preferred.

Toward the "recognition of diversity" end of the continuum is the "accommodationist power sharing" approach to deep division. Four distinct approaches are identified by O'Leary (2013), one of which is consociational. First, centripetalists are the closest of the four to integrationists. They are associated with the work of Donald Horowitz (1985, 2001, 2002) and seek to incentivize convergence to the moderate center ground; they are particularly noted for their advocacy of the "alternative vote" electoral system. They regard this system as encouraging "vote pooling"—forcing ethnic politicians who wish to be electorally successful to seek support from other ethnic groups. This helps "moderate" ethnic parties, who are better placed than extreme ethnic parties to credibly engage in cross-community appeals, to be successful. Multiculturalists go further than centripetalists in terms of embracing the desires of minority groups; they seek to "recognize" and protect distinct minorities and hence support community autonomy and proportionality.

Consociationalists add more protection for minorities. In addition to autonomy and proportionality they advocate cross-community executive power sharing and the provision of veto powers to each community.[1] Hence, a minority group is provided with autonomy over important cultural matters, such as marriage law or education provision, and is proportionately represented in key state institutions such as the police, public service, and parliament (via a proportional electoral system). Further, minorities are included in the executive, which comprises actors from the recognized competing community groups. Also, to pass important legislation it is not a "majority" that is needed but "majorities," namely a majority among each of the recognized communities' elected representatives. This essentially gives a veto power to each community and is a much stronger protection of minorities than other approaches such as a weighted majority in parliament, as weighted majorities give greater power to a large community than a smaller one. This necessity for concurrent community majorities gives each community a veto irrespective of community size, something that the majority community may have difficulty in conceding.

While these four features—inclusive power-sharing executive, veto rights, proportionality, and cultural autonomy—are core elements of the consociational approach, consociations come in different forms (O'Leary 2013). They may be democratic in the (fairly obvious) sense of being derived from free and fair elections, or exist in authoritarian regimes (such as the former Yugoslavia). A consociation may be liberal or corporatist; liberal in the sense that voters are free to vote for whomever they wish at election time, or corporatist in the sense that democratic choice is constrained according to predetermined ascriptive criteria (for example, citizens from community A can only vote for representatives of community A). Consociations may vary according to the level of inclusiveness of the power-sharing executive. A consociational executive may contain all parties in the system—often referred to as a "grand coalition" or a "complete" executive. However, consociations may be highly inclusive rather than all-inclusive: "concurrent" executives contain representatives of the majority of each community, while "plurality" (or "weak") executives contain at least a plurality of each community's representatives. Formal consociations are constitutionally or legally underpinned, while informal ones (for example, the Swiss) rely on convention. Another distinction relates to simple or complex consociations: power sharing in an uncontested territory (simple), or between different peoples who owe allegiance to different nations (complex). A related distinction is between sovereign systems and subsystems of wider polities (i.e., regional consociations).

These distinctions regarding different types of consociations are important as, depending upon the particular case under study, they will shape the precise way the general criticisms of consociation have implications for electoral behavior. The particular types of consociational arrangements operating in the case of Northern Ireland are hence now clarified and, subsequently, their possible implications for electoral democracy in Northern Ireland are specified.

Consociation in Northern Ireland

Almost without exception, analysts agree that Northern Ireland represents a clearly consociational case, containing all four key tenets of consociation, as of the 1998 Agreement, and as revised in the 2006 St. Andrew's Agreement. In relation to proportionality, the electoral system used to elect politicians to the Assembly from which the power-sharing executive is derived is a proportional representation system, ensuring that the Assembly strength of each party—the number of Members of the Legislative Assembly (MLAs) it has—approximates the size of its electoral support. There is proportionality too in key elements of the public service, especially the police, the Police Service of Northern Ireland (PSNI), which replaced the Royal Ulster Constabulary (RUC), which was largely comprised of Protestants.

In relation to the operation of a cross-community power-sharing executive, the Northern Ireland executive is formed using a mathematical formula that ensures that all sizeable parties achieve portfolios. Specifically, a sequential divisor portfolio allocation method (in this case d'Hondt) determines how many portfolios the parties receive and the order in which they choose them. This system of multiparty government formation is very different from the typical coalition generation process, which involves negotiation between parties after the election to agree a "programme for government" and decide how many portfolios each party gets and which particular portfolios are allocated to each party. These negotiations can be difficult and protracted at the best of times and so are not suited to a deeply divided context where the parties from rival identity groups are severely antagonistic toward each other. In such a context the automatic "coalition negotiation" (via d'Hondt) has the advantage of quickly and efficiently achieving a result. According to d'Hondt, whichever party wins the most seats at the Assembly election has first choice of portfolio. That party's seat number is then divided in two, and whichever party now has the highest seat number chooses next. This process continues until all ten portfolios are distributed.

The other key positions to be filled are the co-premier positions: the first minister and deputy first minister, which are formally equal in power. As amended under St. Andrew's Agreement, the leader of the largest party becomes the first minister and the leader of the largest party in the other community becomes deputy first minister.

With respect to the veto rights of each community, the key institutional mechanism relates to "designation." All elected representatives are required to "designate" themselves as either "unionist," "nationalist," or "other." In order for important legislation to pass it must achieve a majority in both designated communities as well as a majority overall. Hence, concurrent majorities are required, which provides both communities with a veto on legislation. (Alternatively, 40 percent in each community and 60 percent overall will suffice.) Finally, with respect to cultural autonomy, this is most obvious in Northern Ireland with respect to education. Although a small number of "integrated" schools operate, most children attend either a Catholic school or (if Protestant) a "state" school.

In addition to these four key criteria (proportionality, autonomy, power-sharing executive, and veto rights), the specific type of consociation operating in Northern Ireland should be specified. As (literally) underlined in Figure 1.1, consociation in Northern Ireland may be characterized as democratic, liberal, formal, complex, regional, and (in the 2007–2011 period under focus in this book) complete. It is democratic in the obvious sense that there are, minor logistical problems aside, free and fair elections to the Northern Ireland Assembly from which the power-sharing executive is derived. It is liberal rather than corporatist in the sense there is a single electoral roll and voters are not categorized according to any particular criteria (specifically Protestant or Catholic, unionist or nationalist). In each constituency all electors receive the same ballot paper and are free to indicate their preferences in any way they like. Also, Northern Ireland operates a "Proportional Representation-Single Transferable Vote" (PR-STV) system for Assembly elections rather than a PR list system. This is of import, as PR-STV gives more freedom and choice to voters to express a range of political preferences. Crucially, for voters who give a first preference vote to a party in their bloc, they are free to give—if they wish—a lower preference vote to a noncommunity party or a party in the opposing community.

Northern Ireland's consociation is complex, in the sense that the consociational settlement sought to resolve an ethnonational dispute between Catholics who identify as Irish and seek unity with the rest of Ireland and Protestants who identify as British and seek union with the rest of the UK. Also, the Northern Ireland arrangement is regional, in the sense that Northern Ireland is not a sovereign state but a devolved consociational administration within the broader UK.

The Northern Ireland power-sharing executive is "complete" (an all-inclusive "grand coalition"), in the sense that all parties in the system are included, in the 2007–2011 Assembly term, in the power-sharing executive. In this parliament, 107 of the 108 MLAs belonged to portfolio-holding parties. Finally, consociation in Northern Ireland is formal, in the sense that the consociational settlement is underpinned by the 1998 Agreement and was ratified by referendum in both parts of Ireland.

In order to assess how electoral democracy operates in this specific Northern Ireland case of consociation I now discuss the general criticisms of consociation, and the general implications of these criticisms for voting behavior under consociation. I specify what these criticisms imply for Northern Ireland, given the particular type of consociation arrangements in operation.

Criticism 1: Consociation Freezes the Underlying Divide

This is a widespread criticism and suggests that consociational arrangements make matters worse. The arrangements solidify the existing deep division, or worse they make a deep division deeper. Consociation does this by recognizing the rival communities/identities and creating a system in which each competing identity group can veto proposals from the rival group. This will, the argument goes, inevitably heighten rather than lessen the salience and political potency of the underlying division. Accordingly, parties in each bloc (each identity group or each community) are incentivized to emphasize their commitment to their community, and voters will vote merely for parties in their community bloc, rather than noncommunity or rival community parties, in order to have as large a political representation as possible for their community (for instance, as many seats as possible in the parliament and the government).

Because of this heightened salience of the underlying ethnic, language, or religious divide, other political issues, not associated with the divide, are suffocated and prohibited from emerging—issues, for example, such as social class and economic issues relating to wealth redistribution, taxation, and spending. Furthermore, "ethnic outbidding" is argued to be a consequence of a rise in the salience of the underlying divide. Within each bloc, parties compete with each other to be the most firm or staunch advocate of their community's position. Hence, "extreme" parties are likely to become popular and electorally successful, while moderate parties will struggle, as they will be portrayed by extreme parties as weak. This ethnic outbidding process is suggested to be fatal for democratic stability in deeply divided places, as the polity is predicted to become ever more polarized and ungovernable (Rabushka and Shepsle 1972). Hence, the prediction is grim for party competition and voting in a consociational

system: because the system heightens the salience of the underlying divide via the recognition of, and allocation of veto powers to, the competing communities, voting is likely to stay within-bloc and increasingly go
to the extreme party in each bloc, leading to spiraling polarization.

Some commentators regard Northern Ireland as an excellent example
of this process. Since 1998 there appears little evidence of cross-bloc voting and very clear evidence of the "extreme" party in each community
bloc becoming more electorally successful. In Figure 1.2 the percentage of
votes won by each party is plotted and shows the rise of Sinn Féin in the
Catholic/Nationalist bloc and the Democratic Unionist Party in the Prot-
estant/Unionist bloc: the "extreme" parties have overtaken the "moderate" parties who initially negotiated the consociational settlement.

However, an opposing view suggests that ethnic outbidding is not
"inevitable" under consociational arrangements (Mitchell et al. 2009).
First of all, parties will only move to more extreme positions if that is
where the voters are. If the extreme position a party adopts is not shared
by many voters, then movement there by a party will not be electorally
successful and will be disincentivized. Also, while consociation may be
seen as heightening or maintaining the salience of the underlying divide,
it arguably does so in a way that encourages extreme parties to moderate.
Assuming voters tend to adopt moderate positions on the underlying
divide, extreme parties who negotiate a consociational power-sharing
settlement will seek as many moderate votes as possible in order to trans-
late these votes into as much executive power as possible. In the liberal
consociation in Northern Ireland, a party's political power in the executive is a direct function of the size of that particular party's electoral support: there is an automatic and proportional linkage of party vote support
to the allocation of executive portfolios, and the co-premiership positions go to the largest party in each bloc. Hence, moves toward the moderate middle rather than the extremes seem rational and appear to best

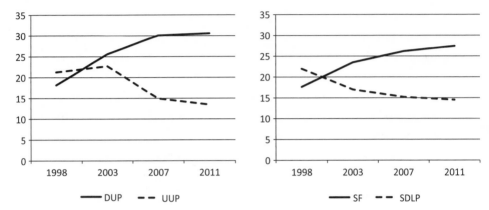

Figure 1.2. Electoral rise of Sinn Féin and DUP and decline of UUP and SDLP at Assembly elections, 1998–2011 (percent of support won at election).

characterize the behavior of the so-called "extreme" parties in Northern Ireland.

For example, Sinn Féin displays a clear historical trajectory from violent irredentist paramilitarism to post-violence acceptance of the legitimacy of Northern Ireland's position in the UK as long as a majority there so desire. The DUP has moved from outright opposition to the 1998 Agreement and refusal to enter government with Sinn Féin to embracing the power-sharing executive. Martin McGuiness, former chief of staff of the Irish Republican Army (IRA), and Ian Paisley, who established the DUP as a bulwark against any compromise to extreme nationalism, became co-premiers in 2007, forming such a good relationship that they were characterized as "the chuckle brothers."[2]

One might expect that this movement by the so-called "extreme" parties toward moderate nationalism and moderate unionism respectively would lead to them to encroach upon the positions of the "moderate" parties in each bloc. The Social Democratic and Labour Party (SDLP) and the

Ulster Unionist Party (UUP), moderate nationalist and unionist parties respectively, negotiated the 1998 Agreement, and their leaders John Hume and David Trimble won the Nobel Peace Prize for this.

In fact, by the 2007 Assembly election commentators identified striking similarities between the parties. McEvoy notes two key related aspects of intra-communal competition in 2007: the institutional incentives for the "extreme" parties to win as many votes and seats as possible and the resulting move to the center ground by these parties.

> In relation to intra-communal competition, both the DUP and Sinn Féin were intent on wiping out the opposition within their respective blocs as they needed the highest number of votes and seats to secure as many ministerial seats as possible under the d'Hondt procedure. It can be argued, however, that the Northern Ireland Assembly election 2007 changed the dynamics of intra-unionist competition between the DUP and the UUP as the former was now supporting power-sharing; it was now a matter of agreeing the schedule of devolution subject to Sinn Féin "delivery" on policing. In terms of intra-nationalist competition, the battleground between the SDLP and Sinn Féin had changed in the wake of the latter's successful ard fheis [party conference] motion on policing. Thus, both the DUP and Sinn Féin had shifted even more onto the "moderate" ground, a process that had been taking place for a number of years. (McEvoy 2007: 372–73)

Similarly, McGarry and O'Leary note that by 2007 both of the unionist parties

> supported inclusive power-sharing, and during the March 2007 elections, unionist and nationalist intra-bloc disagreement was so

minimal that newspapers complained the election was a "hum-drum" affair, and that the election lacked "oomph" because "the extremes had moved to the centre ground, leaving it a very crowded place for the old moderates, the SDLP and the Ulster Unionists." (McGarry and O'Leary 2009: 56)

Socioeconomic and Moral Dimensions?

Hence, it may be that the relative calm, and similarities on the ethnon-ational dimension of the parties, create political space for other political dimensions to become salient, for example, the economic left-right dimen-sion. Sinn Féin has long been characterized as economically left wing, while the SDLP is the more economically centrist of the nationalist par-ties. In the unionist bloc the DUP was established to be to the left of the UUP on economic matters while being more stridently unionist.

McEvoy emphasizes that the apparent absence of within-community competition in the ethnonational dimension seemed to create room for discussion of more "normal" socioeconomic issues and led, for Northern Ireland, to an unusually calm election campaign:

An interesting aspect of the election campaign was the greater discussion on more normal "bread and butter" issues rather than communal positions on the Good Friday/ Belfast Agreement or Northern Ireland's constitutional status. Throughout the cam-paign the parties focused on policy issues such as water rates, corporation tax, health, education and the cost of housing. The media repeatedly reported that the electorate was concerned first and foremost with the prospect of water charges which became the number one issue on the doorsteps. . . . The focus on such issues led commentators to pronounce that the campaign was low-key. . . . For instance, the election was described as "one of the oddest and strangest elections in the history of Northern Ireland" and "a sense of political quiet" had taken hold. (McEvoy 2007: 369)

Wilford and Morrow (2007: 65) describe the campaign as "strangely muted," and Wilford and Wilson (19) similarly comment that "the campaign itself was widely deemed somewhat lacklustre, given that it focused more on 'bread-and-butter' issues than the wider drama of the constitutional status of Northern Ireland." Thus, we may witness consociational arrangements incentivizing "extreme" parties to move to moderate ethnonational positions, hence minimizing ethnonational intra-bloc differences and facilitating non-identity-based party differences to become politically salient, such as social class and economic ideology differences.

Another dimension of competition, in addition to economic left-right, often focused on in international studies of electoral behavior relates to the sociomoral dimension. This distinguishes between social liberals, who hold permissive views on issues such as homosexuality, abortion, and divorce, and social conservatives, who are much more traditionalist. Northern Ireland is generally regarded as a socially conservative context, but there is variation across voters and parties. The DUP is regarded as the most socially conservative, and its long-time leader was head of his own morally fundamentalist (Free Presbyterian) church. Sinn Féin is generally seen as somewhat more liberal than the SDLP. Hence, if intra-community space between parties on the underlying ethnonational divide has lessened, one may investigate if indeed there is any evidence of *either* social class *or* sociomoral intra-community competition.

Variation Across Electoral Context? EU and Electoral Reform Referendum

Another interesting aspect of the freezing hypothesis is to assess whether there is variation across electoral context regarding the importance of the underlying ethnonational divide in driving vote choice. If consociation heightens the salience of the underlying ethnonational divide, does it do so in a way that "infects" the entire polity consistently, irrespective of the precise election at issue? Or, is it just elections to the consociational Assembly that are contaminated by the allegedly heightened salience of the underlying divide caused by the consociational structures? There are two broad schools of thought in the international literature on the salience of issues across electoral contexts. According, to the "second order national election" approach (Reif and Schmitt 1980) all electoral contests in a polity are determined by the same set of issues, irrespective of what the particular contest is "supposed" to focus on. Hence, elections to the European parliament or referendums on specific issues will, instead of being shaped by issues relating to the EU or the referendum, be driven by the "first order" issues relating to the most important electoral contest. This line of argument is consistent with the concern of critics of consociation that ethnonational factors will suffocate all other issues. In contrast to second-order theory, another approach—characterized simply as the "issues approach"—suggests that voters are well able to differentiate between different electoral contexts and rely on different voting criteria depending on the context. Of particular import here is the role played by elections to supra-national authorities. If a consociational polity operates in the context of regional integration, does competition relating to this regional integration potentially cross-cut the underlying divide?

Specifically, Northern Ireland elections to the European Parliament may, in theory at least, be fought on issues relating to EU integration. If so, they may provide an externally generated dimension of competition in the Northern Ireland case to cross-cut the ethnonational dimension of competition. This could, radically, lead to cross-community voting; for example, pro-EU Protestants could vote for the only clearly pro-EU party of the four main parties in Northern Ireland, the "Catholic" SDLP. Or, the EU dimension of competition may influence intra-community voting, particularly in the nationalist bloc, as there is arguably a clear choice between a pro-EU (SDLP) and Euro-skeptic party (Sinn Féin). This highlights the possibility that the strength of the underlying ethnonational dimension in shaping vote choice may vary across electoral context; it may be strongest at elections directly linked to the consociational power-sharing structures (Assembly elections), but face competition from other dimensions of competition at elections to which those dimensions are linked (i.e., the EU dimension at EP elections).

Another potential site for non-ethnonational voting in Northern Ireland is the 2011 referendum on electoral reform. Ostensibly, this referendum arose from disagreements between British political parties regarding the way Westminster elections are conducted. The Liberal Democrats, as part of the coalition formation deal with the Conservatives in 2010, demanded a referendum on the issue of changing the plurality electoral system used for Westminster to a system that they believed was less majoritarian, namely the Alternative Vote. If this issue was simply a debate about the somewhat arcane and abstract merits and demerits of electoral systems advocated by competing British parties, it ought not to—in the Northern Ireland context—be an "ethnonational issue." An alternative reading is that any issue which is essentially a choice between majoritarianism and proportionality is in fact the essence of the ethnonational difference in Northern Ireland, and hence is likely to map squarely onto a unionist-nationalist distinction.[3] In short, it is a matter of empirical investigation to determine the extent to which "second-order" issues such as EP elections and referendums on specific issues, such as electoral reform, are driven by first-order ethnonational concerns. The findings should cast light on the potential of such issue domains in these electoral contexts to achieve salience and cross-cut the ethnonational divide.

Variation Across Party System Context? British and Republic of Ireland Parties

One argument about the dominance of the ethnonational dimension in Northern Ireland politics relates to the particular menu of parties on offer to citizens. The argument of integrationists is that, because the people are offered ethnonational parties at election time, they choose ethnonational parties. If they were offered other types of parties they would choose them instead. This is analogous to saying that if we observe a restaurant full of people eating meat we should not infer that the customers want to eat meat: if vegetarian options had been included in the menu we might have observed much lower levels of meat eating. Plausibly, British parties could compete in Northern Ireland as could, somewhat less plausibly but still possibly, Republic of Ireland parties. Under this counterfactual situation (British and Irish parties competing) we may investigate whether voting behavior is still driven by ethnonational factors, or, as some integrationists have argued, would be driven by more "progressive" issue areas, such as social class and economic left-right views.

Two chapters of this book are devoted to empirically examining the implications of the "freezing" criticism. Chapter 2 examines the strength of ethnonational issues in driving vote choice, assesses whether economic, social, or EU-related issues are important in influencing voting, and investigates whether voting in the AV referendum maps onto, or is distinct from, ethnonational factors. Chapter 3 focuses on potential support for British and Irish parties and examines the extent to which ethnonational and non-ethnonational issues potentially determine support for such parties.

Criticism 2: Consociation Is Undemocratic and Accountability Is Not Possible

Another frequently voiced criticism of consociational arrangements is that they are inherently undemocratic. The argument is that consociation requires all parties in the system to enter a power-sharing executive, and thus the basic Government versus Opposition dichotomy that is a crucial ingredient of a democracy is sacrificed. Accordingly, consociational government takes on some of the unsavory aspects of an authoritarian regime: there is little way to hold the government to account, either by politicians in the system or by citizens.

Politicians cannot effectively scrutinize or criticize the government because all politicians are in the all-inclusive government. The governing parties appear to be a self-serving permanent elite immune from being held to account for their decisions by Opposition politicians, because there is no Opposition. Essentially this criticism says that inclusive government is antithetical to a properly functioning democracy because there is no way to "throw the scoundrels out" and replace the government with a potentially better one.[4]

From the voters' perspective, there is no way to hold the government to account. Voters cannot calculate as follows: the incumbent government has performed poorly, so I will seek to replace the government with a different one. Critics say that a consociational government after an election looks inevitably the same as the one before the election, because all the same parties will be in it. This fatally undermines the key purpose of an election from the citizens' perspective: seeking to ensure that the best parties run the government and the less impressive parties are in opposition.

Proponents of consociation may respond to the charge of being undemocratic by emphasizing that consociations may occur in either authoritarian regimes (such as the former Yugoslavia) or democratic regimes in which there are free and fair elections. Also, within democratic regimes liberal versions of consociation are more democratic than corporatist versions, as they do not constrain voter choice at election time. Also, consociations vary in their use of electoral systems. Proportional representation is a key aspect, but there's an argument between Proportional Representation-Single Transferable Vote (PR-STV) and PR list system. The former offers more choice to voters, as they can fully list their preferences over the candidates on offer. This facilitates the possibility of not only voting for your most preferred party, but indicating preferences for parties that are not your most preferred, for example, parties from the rival community or from none of the rival communities. The Northern Ireland case has free and fair elections, is liberally unconstrained, and uses an electoral system that maximizes choice for the voter (PR-STV). These factors suggest at least a minimal amount of "democracy" at play.

However, what is undoubtedly a challenge for voters in a consociational system is holding the government to account for its performance. Clearly, the government cannot be replaced by an alternative. What can happen, at least in theory, is that the relative size of the constituent parts of the government can change considerably after an election. Intense intra-community competition between governing parties may, in theory at least, be based on relative evaluations of their governing performance. Voters in each bloc are free to "punish" a party for poor performance and reward a party for impressive governing performance. Hence, the standard "reward/punishment" models of voting behavior (e.g., Lewis-Beck 1990) that are used in the international study of elections may well operate.

In theory they can do so; it is a matter of empirical investigation to assess the extent to which they actually do.

Two other (related) features of the Northern Ireland consociational settlement make it especially challenging for voters to hold governing parties to account. The complete nature of the executive and regional nature of the administration serve to maximize the difficulty for voters of assigning political responsibility, the task that underpins the performance-based voting that may hold governing parties to account. In Northern Ireland all parties are included in the executive, resulting in a five-party coalition. There are standard difficulties for citizens in many states which have coalition governments, relating to what is often termed the low "clarity of responsibility" (Powell and Whitten 1993) in the coalition context. In a single-party government it is straightforward to know which particular political party to hold responsible for government decisions: the single governing party. In a two-party coalition voters must figure out which of the two to "blame," or whether to "blame" both equally. In a five-party coalition this challenge becomes much harder.

This "horizontal" distribution of power (across the large range of governing coalition parties) is matched in the multilevel governance case with a vertical distribution of power. In a devolved regional Assembly such as Northern Ireland's the voter must assess what it is that the regional government is actually responsible for before then allocating responsibility to one or other of the five governing parties. Hence, Northern Ireland provides an extremely (horizontally and vertically) challenging case for the investigation of performance-based voting under consociational conditions.

Insofar as there is any evidence of accountability-based (performance-based) voting it may be of a general nature or issue specific. When broken down by issues these issues may be categorized as either "ethnonational" ("conflict-related issues") or non-ethnonational (non-conflict or postconflict-related issues). Ethnonational issues may relate to group representation, policing, or maintenance of peace and stability, while non-ethnonational issues may include economic performance and the performance of key public services such as the health service. Mitchell et al. (2009) argue that group representation is likely to be particularly important. Once a consociational settlement has been agreed by all the main parties in the system, valence-based voting becomes significant. Voters in each community ask, which of the parties representing my community can most robustly defend the interests of my community in the power-sharing executive? Parties' past issue positions on the underlying conflict dimension will inform voters' assessments. For example, Protestants' assessments of the relative ability of the DUP and UUP to staunchly defend the interests of Protestants in the executive will be shaped by the fact that the DUP, until recent years, was an "extreme" unionist party, while the UUP was relatively moderate: the DUP's formerly hawkish position will lead to Protestants calculating that it, rather than the UUP, is best placed to be a robust defender of their interests. The formerly hardline Sinn Féin party will similarly be seen by Catholics as being more competent at defending Catholic interests than the moderate SDLP.

Performance Voting Across the Divide?

This line of argument, that prior ideological position informs current reputation regarding performance,[5] is relevant for understanding how citizens may potentially vote as well as how they currently actually vote. In order to understand the potential for electoral behavior in a fully functioning consociational system to evolve from a situation in which citizens vote for parties from "their" community to a situation in which citizens may vote for a party from the "rival" community, it is necessary to investigate how likely it is that citizens would ever vote for a rival-bloc party and what the factors are that would induce them to do so.

An aspect of performance-based voting is investigated whereby citizens' likelihood of voting for a rival party is related to citizens' assessments of the ability of the rival party to perform the function of looking after the interests of all communities. The issues-valence linkage is relevant here as follows. In the same way as for Sinn Féin and the DUP, being historically extreme leads to parties being perceived as competently able to represent their respective communities, being historically moderate, for the SDLP and UUP, arguably gives them a valence advantage in terms of being perceived as credible and able to represent all communities in Northern Ireland. The notion of the potential vote allows us to engage in counterfactual thinking: would citizens in community A ever vote for parties in community B and, if so, under what conditions. This analysis provides an insight into the malleability of the system and a sense of how there may occur a transition of voting behavior from current within-community space to potentially cross-community space.

Two chapters of this book are devoted to empirically examining the implications of the "undemocratic and unaccountable" criticism. Chapter 4 examines the extent to which voters hold the parties in the Northern Ireland executive to account for their performance. Chapter 5 investigates how Northern Ireland voters may potentially support cross bloc parties based on perceived ability to perform well in terms of representing all groups in society.

Criticism 3: Consociation Is Elite-Driven and Discourages Participation

In addition to allegedly freezing the underlying division and prohibiting accountability, a third criticism of consociational arrangements is that they are elitist and do not encourage citizen participation. The views of civil society groups and ordinary citizens are of lower importance than

the views of leaders of the main parties (and violent groups). Elites negotiate behind closed doors, thereby tainting the entire system as unrepre-
sentative and antithetical to the views of ordinary people. An implication
of this criticism is that political apathy among the population is likely to
grow and that participation levels at election time are, accordingly, likely
to be low. A retort to this criticism from pro-consociationalists is that
consociational arrangements are elitist in the sense that it is party elites
that negotiate a compromise which may include power sharing. In order
to achieve security and order via a consociational settlement, it is un-
avoidable that the leaders of the antagonistic groups are the focus of negotiations. However, the result of the elite negotiations may well be put to
the people for approval in a referendum, as occurred in both parts of Ireland after the 1998 Agreement.

Whether the elite focus results in citizen disengagement at election
time is particularly pertinent in the Northern Ireland case, as turnout
levels have decreased considerably between the first Assembly election in
1998 and the 2011 election. Is disaffection with political parties driving
this lack of participation? One possibly valuable way to investigate this is
to focus on the psychological relationships between voters and parties.
Such relationships between parties and voters are usually discussed in
terms of the extent to which a voter "identifies with" (i.e., feels close to)
a party (Campbell et al. 1960). In the deeply divided context, it may be
useful to think of the psychological relationship as possibly multiple and
negative: for example, I feel distant from all of the parties in my community bloc. If the elite orientation of consociation disempowers citizens, we
might expect it to do so via the mechanism of multiple negative party
identification.

Or, abstention may be rational rather than emotional. One possible
explanation of declining turnout may be directly related to concerns

regarding the difficulty of holding parties and the power-sharing executive to account at election time. If citizens face considerable difficulty in assigning responsibility given the vertical (multilevel government) and horizontal (all-inclusive coalition) distribution of power, one response is to give up entirely and simply abstain at election time. Here, participation levels are seen as the victim of the sharing of power, across parties and across levels of government. These issues, the psychology and the rationality of abstention, are empirically examined in Chapter 6.

Overall Aim of the Book

This book examines voting behavior in the 2007–2011 period in Northern Ireland, a period including the 2007 and 2011 Assembly elections, the 2009 European Parliament election, the 2010 Westminster election, and the 2011 AV referendum. In this historical period of fully functioning consociational government, the determinants of electoral behavior of citizens are examined. The three criticisms of consociational arrangements discussed above have testable implications for citizens' behavior. By subjecting these implications to empirical investigation we may provide an overall picture of the quality of electoral democracy in consociational Northern Ireland: the extent to which the ethnonational ideological dimension, rather than economic, moral, or EU dimensions, shapes voting; the extent to which electoral accountability is observable via performance-based voting; and the extent to which accountability difficulties and multiple antipathy to parties shape the decision to abstain. In the concluding chapter the empirical findings are briefly summarized, and their implications for our understanding of voting behavior and for normative assessments of consociational arrangements in Northern Ireland and beyond are discussed.

Data Used

Four election studies that were commissioned and organized by the author form the data for this book. The surveys are post-election representative samples of the adult Northern Ireland population and were conducted either face-to-face or via telephone. A constant set of ethnonational, economic and sociomoral ideology questions, and demographics were included on all surveys, and in addition survey-specific sets of questions were included. The representativeness of the survey samples may be assessed by comparing the survey estimates of real world behavior (turnout and vote choice) to actual real world behavior. The samples may also be compared to other samples, such as the long- running Life and Times social-attitude surveys, to assess the similarity of the distribution of key political attitude variables. This was done for all surveys, and it is demonstrated (see details in Appendix) that the surveys used provide high quality representative samples.

Chapter 2

Ideology and Vote Choice

As elaborated in the previous chapter, critics of consociation argue that power-sharing institutional arrangements heighten the salience of the underlying divide. This leads to elections being fought on ethnonational lines, with voters from each community voting only for parties that explicitly represent "their" community. It also leads, in terms of intra-community party competition, to "ethnic outbidding," whereby an "extreme" party in each bloc successfully markets itself as the firmest advocate of the community's political positions, and moderate parties consequently suffer electoral decline. According to this line of argument, the ethnonational dimension drives all aspects of politics in a consociation, leaving no room for other issue dimensions to play a role. This chapter empirically investigates the extent to which the ethnonational dimension drove electoral behavior in the 2007–2011 period of fully functioning all-inclusive consociational power sharing in Northern Ireland. Four types of analysis are conducted. First, using a pooled 2007–2011 dataset that combines voting behavior from four separate elections (the 2007 and 2011 Assembly elections, the 2010 Westminster election, and the 2009 European Parliament election), the extent to which ethnonational factors drive vote choice is investigated. Second, again using the pooled dataset, the roles of economic and sociomoral dimensions of competition are examined. Third, the possibly important role of the EU dimension is examined, specifically focusing on the 2009 European Parliament election. Fourth, the referendum on the Alternative Vote electoral system for Westminster elections, held in 2011, is focused on in order to assess whether voting on this ostensibly non-ethnonational issue was in fact driven by ethnonational factors. These analyses allow us to answer, in the specific Northern Ireland context, this general question: is, as critics suggest, electoral behavior in a consociation inevitably and consistently driven by the ethnonational dimension? Or do other issue areas (relating to economic and social factors, regional integration, or electoral reform) break through the alleged ethnonational barrier and become politically salient?

Ethnonational Ideology

The percentage of voters from each religious community who vote for parties explicitly representing their community (Sinn Féin or SDLP in the "nationalist bloc" and the DUP and UUP in the "unionist" bloc) is reported in Table 2.1. A very high proportion of Catholics (93 percent) vote within-bloc, while 84 percent of Protestants vote for a unionist party. The lower Protestant figure is accounted for by the fact that 12 percent of Protestants vote for the cross-community Alliance party, compared to only 5 percent of Catholics who do so. Of the 5 percent of Protestants who vote for a nationalist party, almost all support the SDLP rather than Sinn Féin (Table 2.2). Protestant support for the SDLP looks nontrivial when expressed as a percentage of the party's overall support base. Hence, as reported in Table 2.3, 11 percent of SDLP voters are Protestant. This contrasts with the religious profiles of the DUP and UUP (only 2–3 percent Catholic) and Sinn Féin (only 2 percent Protestant). Of the four main parties, the SDLP is the least religiously homogeneous: 83 percent dominated by one religion, while Sinn Féin, DUP, and UUP are between 93 and

Table 2.1. Religion by Party Bloc Choice (%)

	Protestant	Catholic
Alliance	11.8	4.8
Unionist party	83.7	2.8
Nationalist party	4.5	92.5

Table 2.2. Religion by Party Choice (%)

	Protestant	Catholic
Alliance	11.7	4.8
DUP	52.7	1.9
UUP	31.0	1.0
SF	1.1	60.9
SDLP	3.4	31.5

Table 2.3. Proportion of Party Voters from a Particular Religion (%)

	All.	DUP	UUP	SDLP	SF
Protestant	63.3	92.9	94.1	11.1	2.1
Catholic	22.1	2.8	2.4	83.2	95.5
other	11.6	4.3	3.6	5.7	2.4

96 percent dominated by one religion. The distinctiveness of the SDLP will be returned to in Chapter 5 when the ability of each party to potentially attract support from the "rival" community is assessed. For now, we note that each bloc is strongly religiously based.

While religion membership is an extremely strong signifier of ethnonational position, ethnonationalism is examined here as a set of ideas, not to be conflated with a demographic trait. Figure 2.1 illustrates a simple

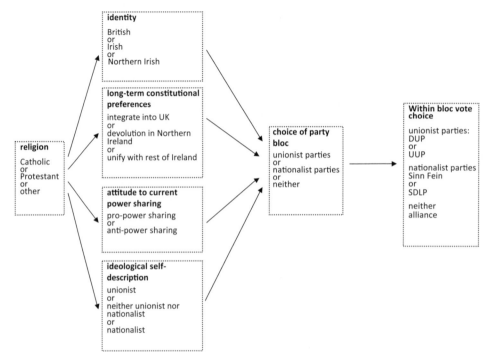

Figure 2.1. Ethnonational model of party choice.

model of voting in which four distinct but related elements of ethnonationalism influence voting behavior. Identity and constitutional preferences are typically seen as the crucial elements of ethnonationalism in Northern Ireland. Crudely, citizens who see themselves as "British" and seek to have Northern Ireland firmly integrated into the rest of the UK are characterized as "unionist," while citizens who feel "Irish" and desire the unification of Northern Ireland with the rest of Ireland are "nationalist." It is crucial, however, to characterize each of these components of ethnonationalism as being made up of three rather than two categories.

Cairns, for example, suggests that "there is encouraging evidence emerging from Northern Ireland that a common or shared in-group identity is beginning to develop" (2013: 285). This "Northern Irish" identity may represent an overarching or superordinate identity which is distinct from "British" and "Irish," a "national-political identity that can be embraced by both Catholics and Protestants" (285). Hayes et al. (2006) and Cairns et al. (2006) suggest that having attended school in an integrated education context is one predictor of adults holding a "Northern Irish" identity. Here the focus is on the political consequences of such an identity. If "Northern Irish" acts as a "neutral" or cross-community identity, this may lead to politically moderate views and behavior. A different interpretation of "Northern Irish" as identity choice is that it may be simply another manifestation of the two main identities. Some Protestants may adopt the term as a way of expressing their belonging to a particular part of the UK, while some Catholics may use it to indicate their belonging to the Northern part of Ireland (see discussion in McKeown 2014). Accordingly, Northern Irish Catholics and Northern Irish Protestants may be just as different from each other as Irish Catholics and British Protestants are. A third possibility is that being "Northern Irish" is a meaningful distinction for Catholics but not for Protestants. As the majority culture, Protestants may "project" their identity on the superordinate "Northern Irish" identity (Noor et al. 2008; Noor et al. 2010; and discussion in McKeown 2014). This would lead to greater voting behavior implications of Northern Ireland identity choice for Catholics than Protestants.

In terms of long-term constitutional preferences, the simple "stay in the UK versus Irish unity" dichotomy has formed the basis of much analysis (see Coakley 2007), but this dichotomy must be relaxed to accommodate the three main contemporary options: Irish unity, full integration into the UK, or devolution within it. The last option characterizes the status quo, and its inclusion helps distinguish within unionism between integrationists and devolutionists. Within the Catholic community this three-way categorization facilitates distinguishing those Catholics who want neither direct rule nor Irish unity.

The terms "nationalist" and "unionist" are ubiquitous in Northern Ireland debates; formally this ideological self-description is politically crucial vis-a-vis the designation process in the Assembly. In terms of citizens' self-description the terms are potentially politically important but must be supplemented with a third possible self-description: "neither unionist nor nationalist." This allows us to distinguish within each community between those who see themselves as part of the political project of their community and those who do not: distinguishing Catholics who are "nationalist" from those who are not and distinguishing Protestants who are "unionist" from those who are not. In addition to identity, long-term constitutional preferences, and ideological self-description, a final element of ethnonationalism focused on here relates to attitudes to the all-inclusive power-sharing government. This is a particularly crucial distinction within the Protestant community, distinguishing between citizens who are very reluctant to share power with Sinn Féin and citizens who accept power sharing with Sinn Féin.

From the pooled election studies 2007–2011 the distribution of responses on these four elements of ethnonationalism is now described, and is broken down by religion to assess within-community variation. Regarding identity, Figure 2.2 shows the proportion of citizens who describe themselves as "British," "Irish," or "Northern Irish." The last option is chosen by 29 percent, more than "Irish," which is chosen by a quarter of respondents, while over two-fifths indicate that they are "British." When identity choice is broken down by religion there is, unsurprisingly, a strong relationship between being Protestant and feeling British, and between being Catholic and regarding oneself as Irish. What is striking, however, is the even distribution of "Northern Irish"

a. All respondents

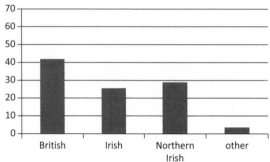

b. Protestants only

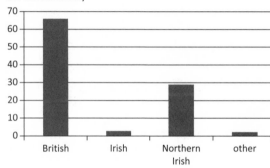

c. Catholics only

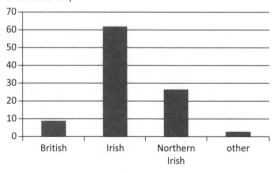

Figure 2.2. National identity.

a. All respondents

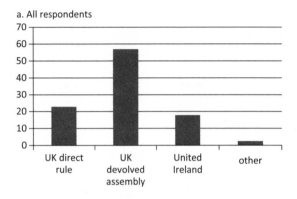

b. Protestants only

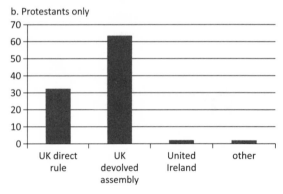

c. Catholics only

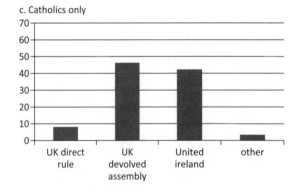

Figure 2.3. Preferred long-term constitutional future.

across the religions; 27 percent of Catholics and 29 percent of Protestants feel "Northern Irish."

In relation to long-term preferences on the constitutional future of Northern Ireland, the largest category is the status quo, remaining in the UK with a devolved administration and Assembly. Almost a quarter want "direct rule," or full integration into the UK, and less than one-fifth wish for a united Ireland. Unsurprisingly, when this is broken down by religion we find that almost no Protestants want a united Ireland; by two to one they desire devolution over integration. For Catholics, a minority seek a united Ireland. Overall, there is solid cross-community support for the long-term Northern Ireland status being devolution within the UK, with about a third of Protestants wanting full (UK) union and just less than half of Catholics wanting full (Irish) unity.

Regarding power sharing, a very large majority support the decision to establish an inclusive power-sharing government in 2007, with only 13 percent opposed. There is variation across community, with, however, almost a fifth of Protestants opposed compared to only 6 percent of Catholics. In relation to ideological self-description, about one-third of the population regard themselves as "unionist" and one-fifth as "nationalist." More than 40 percent describe themselves as "neither unionist nor nationalist." Unsurprisingly, a majority of Protestants see themselves as unionist and a (bare) majority of Catholics see themselves as "nationalist." About two-fifths of each community (slightly less for Protestants and slightly more for Catholics) describe themselves as "neither unionist nor nationalist."

One would expect that positions on each of these four ethnonational factors would be related to each other. Protestants who are British would be expected also to be "unionist," not overly enthusiastic about sharing power, and in favor of full integration into the UK in the long term. Similarly, the various facets of nationalism should cohere.

a. All respondents

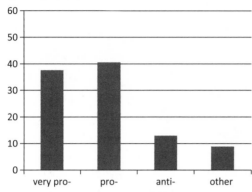

b. Protestants only

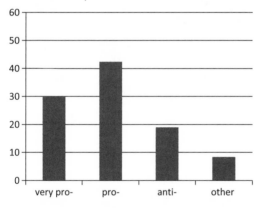

c. Catholics only

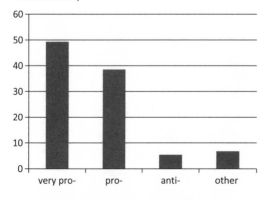

Figure 2.4. Attitudes to power sharing.

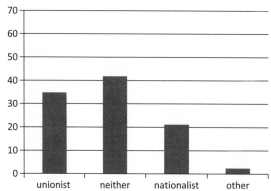

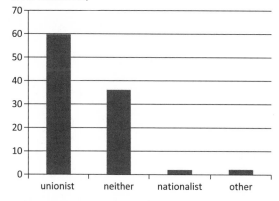

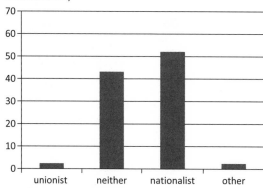

Figure 2.5.
Ethnonational
ideological
self-description.

Table 2.4. Relationship Between Identity and Other Ethnonational Positions

	Protestants		Catholics	
	British	Northern Irish	Irish	Northern Irish
unionist	67.7	51.4	1.1	2.1
neither	31.1	47.0	29.9	63.7
nationalist	1.2	1.6	69.0	34.2
UK direct rule	38.9	23.0	4.6	9.0
UK assembly	60.4	74.8	36.1	70.2
united Ireland	0.6	2.2	59.2	20.8
very pro-power sharing	30.7	36.1	52.8	53.2
pro-power sharing	45.3	49.8	41.2	41.9
anti-power sharing	24.0	14.0	6.0	4.9

In Table 2.4 we assess this hypothesis, and begin with how identity relates to other factors. We find that "British" Protestants are different from "Northern Irish" Protestants: less than a quarter of the latter favor direct rule, compared to two-fifths of the former. Identity-based differences in constitutional preferences are even more stark for Catholics: support for a united Ireland is three times as great among "Irish" Catholics (59 percent) as among "Northern Irish" Catholics (21 percent). The "British" versus "Northern Irish" distinction among Protestants also differentiates Protestants who are "unionist" and those who are not: "British" Protestants are "unionist" by a proportion of 2 to 1, while "Northern Irish" Protestants are almost evenly divided between "unionists" and "neither unionist nor nationalist." An analogous, but much starker, pattern emerges among Catholics. "Irish" Catholics are over twice as likely to be nationalist as "neither unionist nor nationalist," while "Northern Irish" Catholics are almost twice as likely to be "neither unionist nor nationalist" as "nationalist." The identity distinction is related to attitudes to power sharing among Protestants: one-quarter of "British" Protestants are opposed, compared to only 14 percent of "Northern Irish" Protestants. Among Catholics, attitudes to power-sharing are equally positive, irrespective of identity. This analysis of the relationship between identity choice and other facets of ethnonational positions suggests that the "Northern Irish" identity is politically meaningful, in the sense that it is related to relatively moderate aspects of ethnonationalism within both communities, but particularly so within the Catholic community, seemingly echoing the asymmetric findings of Noor et al. (2008).

The other relationships between the aspects of ethnonationalism are now examined. The relationship between ideological self-description and long-term constitutional preferences shows that Protestants who are unionist are more likely than Protestants who are "neither unionist nor nationalist" to support direct rule: almost two-fifths of the former compared to one-quarter of the latter (Table 2.5). A much stronger pattern emerges for Catholics. Nationalist Catholics are much more supportive of a united Ireland (60 percent) than "neither unionist nor nationalist" Catholics are (25 percent). Also, "unionists" are more strongly opposed to power sharing than non-unionist Protestants, and the pro-power-sharing position of Catholics is stronger for "nationalists" than non-nationalists. Finally, we compare current and future constitutional preferences (Table 2.6). Catholics who in the long term desire a united Ireland are just as happy, if not happier, with current power sharing as Catholics who desire the long-term future to be devolution within the UK. There is a strong relationship within the Protestant community; those whose long-term desire is

Table 2.5. Relationship Between Ideological Self-Description and Power Sharing and Constitutional Future

	Protestants		Catholics	
	"unionist"	*"neither"*	*"neither"*	*"nationalist"*
UK direct rule	37.9	26.5	13.1	4.0
UK assembly	61.4	70.1	61.6	36.4
united Ireland	0.6	3.4	25.3	59.7
very pro-power sharing	27.1	40.0	49.3	55.3
pro-power sharing	47.7	46.1	45.9	38.0
anti-power sharing	25.1	13.8	4.8	6.6

Table 2.6. Relationship Between Constitutional Preferences and Attitudes to Power Sharing

	Protestants		Catholics	
	direct rule	Assembly	united Ireland	Assembly
very pro-power sharing	21.9	36.5	53.6	50.9
pro-power sharing	48.9	46.3	42.1	42.1
anti-power sharing	29.2	17.2	4.3	6.9

devolution within the UK are over twice as likely to be very pro-power sharing as anti-power sharing, while in contrast "direct rule" Protestants are more likely to be anti-power sharing than very pro-power sharing.

Overall, these four aspects of ethnonationalism are related to each other in coherent ways, and the distribution of opinion on these factors suggests that three-way categorizations are much more appropriate than regarding distinctions as dichotomous (British/unionists versus Irish/

nationalists). In fact, the neutral categories are highly populated: the biggest ideological self-description category is "neither unionist nor nationalist," current power sharing and long-term devolution are strongly supported, and "Northern Irish" is a sizeable identity choice. It may be reasonable to see the political distinctions in each community as operating, not between moderate ethnonationals and extreme ethnonationals, but rather between citizens who are ethnonationally neutral and those who are ethnonationally committed. In terms of the distribution of ethnonational opinion the large proportions of "neutral" or "moderate" citizens in the overall population and in each community are not consistent with the fears of critics of consociation that the views of citizens under consociation will look strongly ethnonationally polarized. In contrast, the overall picture is support for the inclusive power-sharing accommodation and devolved government in the long term, and the most prevalent self-description is "neither unionist nor nationalist."

Can these distinctions on long-term constitutional future, national identity, ideological self-description, and attitudes to power sharing help us understand within-community vote choice? Is there a clear distinction in the voting behavior of (to use the ubiquitous terms) "hardliners" and "moderates" in each community? Are moderate Protestants more likely than staunchly unionist Protestants to support the DUP rather than the UUP? Are hardline nationalists more likely to support Sinn Féin rather than the SDLP?

In Table 2.7 Protestant vote choice between the DUP and UUP is examined. The results are easy to interpret: there are no strong relationships between the four factors and vote choice (none reach statistical significance). DUP voters are essentially no different from UUP voters on these four factors. This is in sharp contrast to the patterns than emerge for Catholic vote choice between Sinn Féin and the SDLP (Table 2.8). Catholics who are "Irish" strongly support Sinn Féin rather than SDLP, by

Table 2.7. Protestant Vote Choice Between DUP
and UUP by Ethnonational Position

	DUP	UUP
British	62.1	37.9
Northern Irish	65.9	34.1
Direct rule	60.7	39.3
Assembly	64.2	35.8
very pro-	61.0	39.0
pro-	61.5	38.5
anti-	67.8	32.2
unionist	63.1	36.9
neither unionist/nationalist	60.9	39.1

Table 2.8. Catholic Vote Choice Between Sinn
Féin and SDLP by Ethnonational Position

	SDLP	SF
Irish	25.2	74.8
Northern Irish	52.3	47.1
united Ireland	13.9	86.1
Assembly	53.8	46.2
very pro-	36.4	63.6
pro-	31.7	68.8
anti-	30.6	69.4
nationalist	26.7	73.3
neither unionist/nationalist	49.0	51.0

a proportion of three to one, whereas "Northern Irish" Catholics are evenly divided between Sinn Féin and the SDLP. A similar, and even stronger, pattern emerges in relation to constitutional preferences. Almost all Catholics in favor of a united Ireland vote Sinn Féin rather than SDLP, whereas a slight majority of Catholics who support staying in the

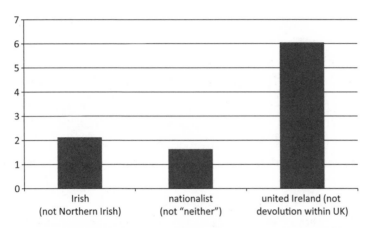

Figure 2.6. Strength of influence of intra-Catholic ethnonational distinctions on vote choice between SDLP and Sinn Féin (2007–2011 pooled election studies). Bars indicate the odds ratios from a logistic regression using identity, ideological self-description, and constitutional preferences to predict Sinn Féin rather than SDLP vote choice (controlling for age, year of survey, sex, and social class. For instance, the chance of an "Irish" (rather than "Northern Irish") Catholic supporting Sinn Féin is just over twice as great as the chance of an "Irish" (rather than "Northern Irish") Catholic supporting the SDLP.

UK with a devolved government support SDLP rather than Sinn Féin. Also, "nationalist" Catholics support Sinn Féin (three to one), whereas Catholics who are "neither unionist nor nationalist" are evenly divided between Sinn Féin and SDLP. No relationships emerge regarding power sharing, perhaps not surprisingly as this is an issue that separates strong from moderate unionists whereas both nationalist parties strongly favor it.

In order to assess the relative strength of the different aspects of ethnonationalism in predicting Catholic choice between Sinn Féin and the SDLP, a regression analysis was conducted. Figure 2.6 illustrates the important predictors. The identity and ideological self-description distinctions are influential, but long-term constitutional preferences are crucial. The chance of a "united Ireland" Catholic supporting Sinn Féin (rather than

SDLP) is six times greater than the chance of a "pro-devolution" Catholic supporting Sinn Féin rather than SDLP.

As far as the Alliance is concerned, the data in Tables 2.1–2.3 suggest that the party's policy of attracting significant levels of support from both communities is successful, but the overall balance is significantly in favor of Protestants rather than Catholics. Table 2.9 reports that Alliance does particularly well among "neither unionists nor nationalists," getting 20 percent support from that group. The highest support within the identity categories is from "Northern Irish," and within the constitution categories is "Assembly and devolution." Hence, Alliance support comes from the "neutral" ethnonational categories. However, in each case it is the "unionist" rather than "nationalist" category which is next highest; the party attracts few Irish identifiers or supporters of a united Ireland or "nationalists." This suggests an overall description, in tune with many commentators, of mild unionism.

The strong ethnonational basis to Sinn Féin versus SDLP vote choice, the absence of such a basis to DUP-UUP vote choice, and the mildly unionist support base of Alliance may be illustrated by comparing the position of party voters on an ethnonational scale. To generate this scale, the four aspects of ethnonationalism are added together; the scale runs from the most nationalist position possible to the most unionist position possible. Figure 2.7 plots the average position of party voters on the scale. This shows the UUP and DUP on the same spot, and Sinn Féin to the nationalist side of the SDLP, with Alliance somewhat on the unionist side of the graph. This graph is repeated (Figure 2.8), but this time with distance from the center point illustrated. This shows that the Catholic-bloc parties flank the unionist parties. Regarding the four main parties, the overall picture in terms of voter positions is of UUP and DUP sameness and moderate SDLP versus hardline Sinn Féin.

Table 2.9. Ethnonational Support Base of
Alliance (%)

Protestant	11.8
Catholic	4.8
Other	23.6
British	11.3
Irish	2.5
Northern Irish	12.4
Direct Rule	9.3
Devolved Assembly	11.7
United Ireland	2.4
Very pro-power sharing	11.8
Pro-power sharing	8.7
Anti-power sharing	3.0
Unionist	6.5
Neither	19.7
Nationalist	1.6

Hence, there is clear cross-community asymmetry: marked differences between the support base of nationalist parties and identical support bases of the unionist parties. This may be explained by the fact
that interparty divisions in the former bloc have always been much
deeper than in the latter. The traditional distinction in nationalism was
between a violent (republican) and a constitutional (nationalist) approach
to politics, a distinction largely absent on the unionist side. Coakley
(2008: 779), for example, suggests that

the clash between Sinn Féin and the SDLP is technically more
recent [than the DUP-UUP clash], but its roots lie deep in Irish
history . . . and the difference [s] between the perspectives with
which the parties have traditionally been associated are much

Figure 2.7. Mean voter position for each party on ethnonational scale.

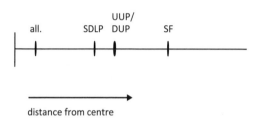

distance from centre

Figure 2.8. Party voter positions: distance from center point of the scale.

more profound than in the case of unionism . . . . It is to be presumed that perspectives on the legitimacy of paramilitary violence play a major role in differentiating Sinn Féin from SDLP supporters.

Also, there appear to be very marked long-term policy differences between the party leaderships. Sinn Féin is wedded to the idea of a united Ireland and sees the Agreement as a stepping stone to this end. The SDLP is much more lukewarm. The long-term constitutional preferences of nationalists, therefore, provide a durable distinction between Sinn Féin and SDLP supporters. An analogous constitution-based debate, between devolutionist unionists and full- integration unionists, lacks potency in the unionist bloc. Thus, while the present policy positions of Sinn Féin and the SDLP may be remarkably similar (both nonviolent and wedded to devolved power sharing within the UK), their pasts (in terms of attitudes to violence) and their prescribed futures (constitutionally) significantly differ, leading to continued strong distinctions between their respective support bases on the ethnonational dimension. In short, as McGarry and O'Leary note (2009: 56), the differences between the DUP and the UUP "have never been stark, and not as wide as those between Sinn Féin and the SDLP."

One may conclude that the findings regarding the ethnonational basis of intra-community vote choice are clear but asymmetric. DUP's movement in the moderate direction and embracement of power sharing with Sinn Féin has led to the disappearance of distinctions between the DUP and UUP on ethnonational positions: the voters of the two parties are essentially indistinguishable. This is not consistent with the fears of critics of consociation that movement in an extreme direction is inevitable, leading—in the Northern Ireland case—to an extremist DUP support base versus a moderate UUP support base. On the nationalist side, however, there are still very clear "hardline" versus "moderate" distinctions in the support bases of the parties. The transition of Sinn Féin from violent irredentists to nonviolent power-sharers within the UK has undoubtedly led to Sinn Féin and the SDLP looking very similar in terms of support for the current institutional arrangements. However, the past and the future serve to distinguish the parties, leading to clearly and strongly identifiable ethnonational distinctions in their support base.

Economic and Sociomoral Dimensions

Is there any evidence of party competition and voting behavior being driven by non-conflict issue areas? In relation to economic left-right issues, Evans and Duffy (1997) note that the DUP was established initially not only to provide a more staunch unionism than the UUP but also to represent working-class Protestant interests: it was to the UUP's left on economics and to the right on ethnonational matters. Similarly, Sinn Féin has a reputation for appealing somewhat more to working-class Catholics than to middle-class Catholics, for whom the SDLP is arguably more attractive. Previous research has empirically identified these social class patterns of intra-bloc party support (for example, Evans and Tonge 2009). Relatedly, the DUP and Sinn Féin have reputations as being more ideologically economically left wing than their respective rivals (UUP and SDLP). In a comprehensive analysis using survey data from 1989 to 2006, Tilley and Evans (2011) found a social class and economic ideology basis to within-community vote, with the DUP being more working class and left wing than the UUP and Sinn Féin being more working class (but not strongly more left wing) than the SDLP.

In Table 2.10 the social class basis of party support is examined, and also, for the purpose of comparing class with other demographic factors, the age and sex basis of voting is presented. The data suggest that the DUP and Sinn Féin attract younger and more working-class voters in their respective communities, but only in relation to Catholic choice, between Sinn Féin and the SDLP, are the differences strong enough to be statistically significant. This is especially so for age: the youngest age category (18-to-24-year-olds) supports Sinn Féin rather than SDLP by a proportion of 3 to 1, whereas support is almost evenly divided between the two parties in the oldest age group (65 plus). In line with expectations, Sinn Féin attracts somewhat more working-class than middle-class support: almost 70 percent of the c2de category and just over 60 percent of the abc1 category, with middle-class Catholics somewhat more likely to support the SDLP.

Figure 2.9 shows the distribution of opinion on taxes versus spending, capturing the underlying divide between those who are right wing on economic matters, hoping for less state intervention, and more left-wing people, desiring a greater role for the state. Northern Ireland citizens, by this measure, are more left wing than right wing although the largest category is "keep as now," a centrist approach. The distribution of

Table 2.10. Vote Choice by Social Class, Age, and Sex

	Protestant choice between DUP and UUP		Catholic choice between SDLP and Sinn Féin	
	DUP	*UUP*	*SDLP*	*SF*
18–24	71.8	28.2	25.4	74.6
25–44	65.8	34.2	29.7	70.3
45–64	61.0	39.0	37.3	62.7
65+	58.7	41.3	46.3	53.7
male	65.9	34.1	35.2	64.8
female	60.5	39.5	33.2	66.8
abc1	60.6	39.4	39.0	61.0
c2de	65.3	34.7	30.8	69.2

Table 2.11. Vote Choice by Economic and Sociomoral Position

	Protestant choice between DUP and UUP		Catholic choice between SDLP and Sinn Féin	
	DUP	*UUP*	*SDLP*	*SF*
less tax/spend	54.4	45.6	32.4	67.6
same	66.7	33.3	32.1	67.9
more tax/spend	59.9	40.1	37.4	62.6
pro-gay rights	62.3	37.7	32.4	67.6
not sure	56.9	43.1	36.3	63.7
anti-gay rights	66.0	34.0	37.8	62.2

opinion is almost the same across Catholic and Protestant respondents. When related to vote choice no clear relationship emerges in either community (Table 2.11).

In addition to discussion of economic differences, previous research has suggested that the "moral" dimension has shaped party support,

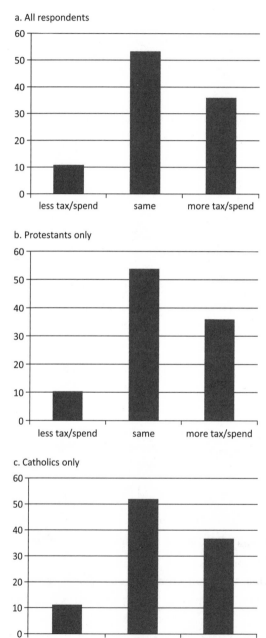

a. All respondents

b. Protestants only

c. Catholics only

Figure 2.9. Attitudes to taxation and spending.

a. All respondents

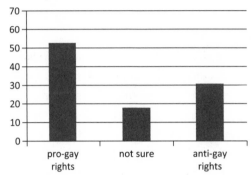

b. Protestants only

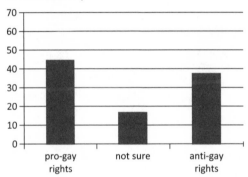

c. Catholics only

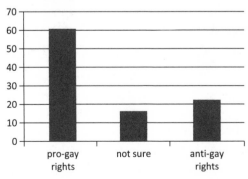

Figure 2.10. Attitudes to homosexuals' rights to marriage and adoption of children.

particularly in the Protestant community. "Social liberals" have relatively permissive attitudes to issues such as abortion, homosexuality, and euthanasia, whereas more authoritarian and traditional attitudes are held by "social conservatives." Mitchell and Tilley (2004) found some evidence that survey respondents' positions on a liberal-conservative value scale significantly predicted DUP versus UUP partisanship, with relatively conservative Protestants preferring the former party (though this relationship is dependent on which particular year was being analyzed (Tilley et al. 2008)). In terms of nationalist party competition, one might expect Sinn Féin supporters to be more secularly and liberally inclined than the relatively morally conservative SDLP supporters (Gilland-Lutz and Farrington 2006). This liberal-conservative distinction is measured in the pooled dataset by focusing on the issue of homosexuality. Northern Ireland citizens emerge as more liberal than conservative on this issue, although there is significant community difference. Protestants are almost evenly divided, whereas Catholics are much more liberal than conservative (Figure 2.10).

Do positions on this issue drive vote choice? No systematic relationship emerges regarding intra-bloc party choice in either community (Table 2.11). Hence, the picture overall is a nationalist bloc with intra-bloc voting that is based strongly on ethnonational differences and to some extent on social class and age but with no evidence of the economic policy or sociomoral policy predicting choice. Party choice in the unionist bloc has no ethnonational basis, no class basis, and no economic or social policy basis.

EU Dimension

Turning now to a potential EU-based dimension of competition, commentators have noted that while interparty differences exist in both blocs the variation is greater in the nationalist bloc, between a strongly pro-European

SDLP and a more skeptical Sinn Féin. McLaughlin (2009: 603), for example, refers to the SDLP as being "generally viewed as the most pro-European party in Ireland" and notes that party members favor the term "European" to describe the party, often ahead of terms such as "nationalist" or "social democratic." The pro-EU position of the SDLP has been identified by an "expert" survey on party positions in Northern Ireland conducted in 2003, with the results placing, by a wide margin, the SDLP as the most pro-EU of the major Northern Ireland parties. Similarly, the SDLP was described as "the champions of European integration in Northern Ireland" on the basis of a 2003 survey of party candidates (Gilland-Lutz and Farrington, 2006: 727). As in preceding European Parliament election campaigns, the SDLP in the 2009 campaign played up its pro-EU credentials. Party leader Mark Durkan stated in the introduction to the party manifesto that the SDLP was "the only major party in the North that is pro-European," and, among other issues in the campaign, the party supported the adoption of the Euro currency in Northern Ireland and the implementation of the Lisbon Treaty (Hainsworth and McCann 2010).

In contrast to the SDLP, Sinn Féin has been markedly critical of the EU. While its Euro-skepticism has moderated over recent years, it retains a predominantly unenthusiastic approach to European integration. Sinn Féin's relationship with the EU, Maillot argues, "has changed significantly since the late 1990s," and the party has "moved from a position of outright opposition to European integration to one of "critical engagement" (2009: 559). Maillot states that Sinn Féin's "cautious engagement" with the EU is "predicated on a careful presentation of itself as a resolutely republican and left wing party," and the role played by the party in EP elections and EU-related referendums is "a self-consciously independent and oppositional one" (2009: 559). This characterization of Sinn Féin as skeptical of integration is consistent with the results of the expert and candidate surveys, in both of which Sinn Féin was substantially less enthusiastic about the EU than was the SDLP. Sinn Féin's 2009 campaign emphasized Irish unity and the party's work for communities on both sides of the border, and much of their campaigning related to building support in Europe for Irish unification. The Sinn Féin campaign included opposition to the Lisbon Treaty, and Sinn Féin had been the only major party in the Republic to oppose the Lisbon Treaty (Hainsworth and McCann 2010: 308–9). Overall, the skeptical tone of the Sinn Féin campaign was consistent with what Maillot notes as "the de facto prioritising of the critical over the engaged elements in Sinn Féin's approach to European integration" (2009: 559).

In the unionist bloc the distinctions between the parties on EU matters are not as great as those between the pro-EU SDLP and skeptical Sinn Féin, although the DUP is generally seen as somewhat more skeptical than the UUP. Murphy (2009) notes that the shared UUP/DUP skepticism has not stopped the UUP "from developing a less hostile approach" (593) and that the party's "traditionally negative approach to the EU has changed over time, shifting from opposition to pragmatism or realism" (589). Murphy suggests that the UUP stance may be summarized as "pragmatic but lacking a wholehearted embrace of fundamental EU principles" (593).

In a similar vein, Ganiel notes that neither of the two main unionist parties "can be described as pro-European, but the DUP conscientiously presents itself as more Eurosceptic than the UUP" (2009: 586). Ganiel notes that what distinguishes the DUP is that core elements of the party's skepticism are "grounded in extreme religious interpretations of the purpose and process of European integration." However, the main focus of the DUP's 2009 election campaign was attaining the most votes and thus depriving the main nationalist party—Sinn Féin—of a poll- topping victory. The DUP candidate, Diane Dodds, stated at the campaign launch,

"Let us not be side-tracked, the top priority for us all at this election must be to stop Sinn Féin from topping the poll" (Hainsworth and McCann 2010: 305). Peter Robinson, DUP leader and First Minister, similarly stated that "I want to make sure that the republican agenda is thwarted" (Hainsworth and McCann, 2010: 306). The urgency of the poll topping issue came from the split within the DUP. The incumbent MEP, Jim Allister, left the DUP in protest over its joining Sinn Féin in government and set up his own party—Traditional Unionist Voice (TUV). In addition to a clearly anti-Sinn Féin position, Allister had a "longstanding Euro-sceptic position," and his antipathy to an integrated Europe gained him the support of the UK Independence Party and some noted Conservative Euro-skeptics (Hainsworth and McCann 2010: 307).

In order to assess the extent to which the EU views of citizens shaped voting in the 2009 European election, a pro-EU versus anti-EU scale was generated, using responses to two questions about the perceived economic benefit of the EU and desire for further integration of the EU. No mean differences between the DUP and UUP voters emerged. However, Sinn Féin voters are more Euro-skeptic than SDLP voters. This asymmetry is consistent with the earlier description of notable party policy differences between the nationalist parties and mild DUP-UUP differences. The question to be addressed is whether attitudes to the EU (a) predict vote choice between Sinn Féin and the SDLP and (b) do so to a stronger extent in the EU election than in a non-EU election. Are non-ethnonational issues (such as regional integration) more likely to be salient in the context of a particular election in which they are supposed to be important (such as a European Parliament election)? Or, consistent with criticisms of consociation, will the heightened salience of the ethnonational divide lead ethnonationalism to "contaminate" all elections? This latter interpretation is consistent with the second-order national election study interpretation of European Parliament elections, which sees such elections as not about the EU but rather as mere electoral extensions of national politics. In the post-election datasets used in this book, it is only in relation to the EP election 2009 and the Westminster election 2010 that the EU attitude scale, described earlier, is available. Hence, we now compare the extent to which EU views drive SDLP-SF voting behavior across these two elections. A regression analysis using the pooled 2009/2010 data was conducted in which the explanatory power of the EU issue was identified, while controlling for ethnonational factors (in the form of a summed ethnonational scale) (Appendix A1). As illustrated in Figure 2.11, the difference between being fairly pro-EU and fairly skeptical leads to a very sizeable increase in the probability of voting Sinn Féin (rather than SDLP) in the European Parliament election, but there is essentially no effect in the Westminster election.

The implication of these findings is that regional integration projects may add a new layer of political competition onto preexisting national level party competition. In a deeply divided society this additional "new" dimension may serve to "normalize" political competition, in the sense of increasing the role of non-conflict-related party competition and voter behavior. The relationship between regional integration projects (such as the EU) and deeply divided societies (such as Northern Ireland) is often discussed in terms of the direct help the former can give the latter to aid progress toward a peaceful, stable, and prosperous society (for example, McCall and O'Dowd 2008). The "help," as indicated here, may also be indirect—in terms of adding a layer of political competition to preexisting ethnonational competition and ensuring the non-dominance of the underlying political conflict cleavage in driving vote choice.

Hence, consociational arrangements do not appear to completely suffocate political competition and render it perpetually driven by issues relating to the underlying conflict cleavage. The findings suggest that when political parties in deeply divided societies offer substantially different

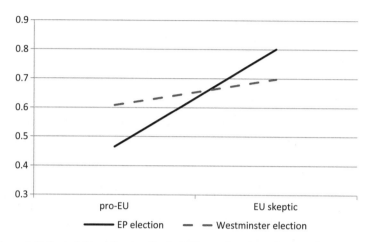

Figure 2.11. Probability of voting for Sinn Féin rather than SDLP, given different views on EU integration and different electoral contexts. The graph shows that skeptics are much more likely than pro-EU voters to support Sinn rather than SDLP, but only at the European Parliament election. (On the 7-point 0–6 scale pro-EU is "1" and EU skeptic is "4," marginally more than a movement from one standard deviation below the mean to one standard deviation above the mean; graph calculated from logistic regression results in Appendix A.)

positions on a particular "new" policy dimension (i.e., a non-conflict-based dimension) and hence offer a clear opportunity for voters to choose between them, voters do respond by voting on the basis of that dimension, but only when the electoral context makes that issue at least somewhat salient. It is to a different electoral context—the referendum context—that attention is now turned to assess whether this context facilitates the emergence of non-conflict voting.

Referendum on the Alternative Vote Electoral System

In 2011 the British Liberal Democrats achieved their wish of having a referendum on the electoral system for Westminster elections. The party's priority was full-blown proportional representation, but they feared this would not have a chance of succeeding, and the party's coalition partner— the Conservatives—were against offering it as an option. Thus the Liberal Democrats advocated the Alternative Vote (AV) as a replacement of the existing plurality system. Hence Northern Ireland, as did the rest of the UK, voted on the issue in a referendum in 2011. Ironically enough, the AV electoral system has featured prominently in academic debates regarding the merits of consociation. Particularly, the AV system is, as noted earlier, preferred by centripetalists, and most notably Donald Horowitz. Under AV there are single seat constituencies, and voters rank order the candidates. To win, a candidate must achieve the support of a majority of voters, either from first preferences or—if no one achieves a first- preference majority—from lower preferences of unsuccessful candidates which are distributed. It is the need to attract lower-preference votes which is attractive to centripetalists, as they see this as incentivizing ethnic leaders to be moderate and appeal across the ethnic divide. Others see this as flawed, as AV will only incentivize moderation under limited circumstances. It is, after all, a majoritarian system; in constituencies in which one ethnic group is a majority, that ethnic group will likely achieve all the representation for that constituency. This contrasts with multi-member constituencies, which leads to representation for all sizeable groups in a given constituency, though this feature encourages, centripetalists believe, the flourishing of small extreme parties.

This AV versus PR debate did not gain headlines in the AV campaign, and AV was advocated as a proportional system (even though it is a variation of majoritarian systems). However, AV would likely lead to a more proportional Westminster than does the status quo. AV was also sold as a system which is likely to lead to coalition government, given that it will be harder for a single party to gain a majority. Hence, those in favor of a change in a more proportional direction supported AV, while those against supported the status quo. What is interesting to observe in the Northern Ireland case is the extent to which ethnonational distinctions map onto voting behavior in this referendum. Despite looking, at face value, like a distinct issue that is of concern to arguments between British political parties, there is good reason to expect ethnonational factors to determine choice between AV and the status quo plurality system. The majoritarian disposition of unionists, traditionally the majority group, contrasts with the proportional disposition of nationalists, typically seen as the minority group. The basis of the 1998 Agreement and the consociational settlement is proportionality and the sharing of power. AV, compared to the existing UK system, was described as a proportional system that would lead to sharing of power (more coalitions at Westminster). Moving to AV is consistent with the proportionality and power-sharing facets of the Northern Ireland system that nationalists support and is inconsistent with the skepticism of power sharing and the fondness for majoritarianism of unionists. The AV referendum in Northern Ireland may then be characterized as an externally generated but not necessarily cross-cutting political issue: the (pro-proportionality) pro-AV arguments and (pro-majoritarian) anti-AV arguments in the referendum campaign arguably map onto the long standing pro-proportionality views of Catholics, who were overwhelmingly supportive of the proportional 1998 Agreement, and skeptical-of-proportionality views of Protestants, who were skeptical of the proportional 1998 Agreement.

Figure 2.12 shows the breakdown of support for the referendum by religion and by ethnonational beliefs. Protestants, by a massive margin, are more likely to vote No than Catholics are. Also, all four of the ethnonational ideological factors are strongly related to voting. Hence, "Irish" voters are least likely to vote No, while "British" are most likely to vote No, and the "Northern Irish" are in between. Similarly, "nationalists" and those who are pro-united Ireland are most distinct from

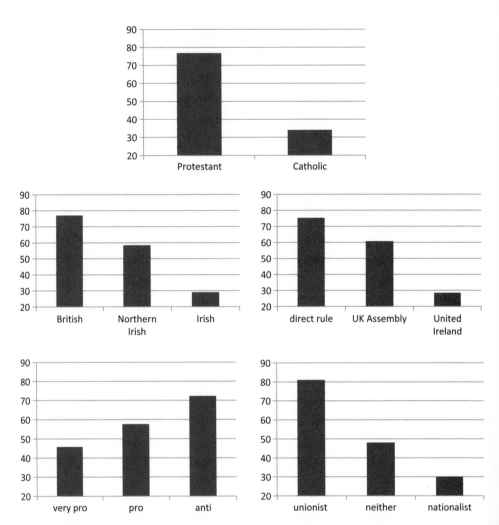

Figure 2.12. Percentage "No" vote in AV Referendum, broken down by religion and ethnonational positions.

"unionists" and those in favor of direct rule. Also, those strongly in favor of sharing power are much less likely than anti-power sharers to vote No.

It is also interesting to investigate referendum voting within each community in order to assess which ethnonational factors most effectively explain within-community variation in voting behavior. What is striking is the significant difference in voting between "Irish" Catholics and "Northern Irish" Catholics, the former being much less likely to oppose AV than the latter. In contrast, the "British" versus "Northern Irish" distinction produces only marginal difference in the Protestant community. Among Protestants it is the distinction between "unionist" and "neither unionist nor nationalist" which provides most explanatory power, the former being more strongly inclined to oppose AV than the latter.

Discussion

Voting in this period (2007–2011) is ethnonational in the sense that party blocs strongly operate. Catholics opt for "Catholic" parties and Protestants opt for "Protestant" ones. The main parties in each bloc have strong religious community profiles, although the SDLP is somewhat distinctive here with its lower level of homogeneity. The attitudinal profile of the population, however, suggests a strongly moderate populace with high levels of support for neutral or non-ethnonational options. Also, the move in a moderate direction by the DUP has led it to encroach firmly onto UUP territory, meaning that ethnonational distinctions between the two parties are marginal. In terms of ethnonational positions the vote base of the two parties is essentially the same. However, the move in a moderate direction by Sinn Féin has not led to an absence of ethnonational differences in the Sinn Féin-SDLP support bases. Ethnonational position strongly drives nationalist vote choice.

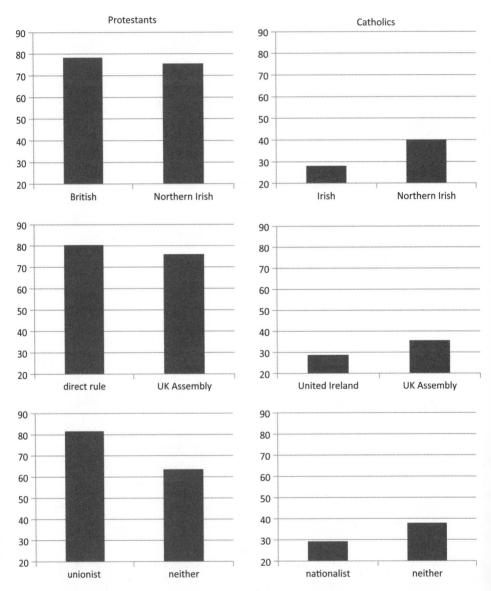

Figure 2.13. Catholic and Protestant vote choice in AV referendum, broken down by ethnonational positions.

If party positions within each bloc are similar on ethnonational issues, has this left political space for social class and economic policy differences to flourish? The short answer is: not much. While a social class
basis to nationalist vote choice is identifiable, there is not a significant
basis in the unionist bloc. Also, while economic ideological differences
were in the expected direction, they were not significant. The very fact
that all the parties are sharing power may make the challenge of developing very distinct economic policy positions difficult. Sociomoral distinctions, while in the expected direction, were not strong. The one issue area
where interesting evidence emerged of a strong role in shaping vote choice
relates to the EU. In the EP election attitudes to regional integration
(controlling for ethnonational factors) quite strongly predict vote choice
between SDLP and Sinn Féin; this EU effect is much larger at the EP
election than at a non-EP election—specifically in the analysis, a Westminster election. This suggests that, as in many EU countries, debate over
the EU can play an important role in driving vote choice, even in the
challenging context of Northern Ireland. Another externally generated
electoral contest had the opposite effect: the AV referendum mapped
very strongly onto ethnonational distinctions. This suggests that the potential for other electoral arenas to generate non-ethnonational voting is
very context dependent.

Chapter 3

Ideology and Potential Support for British and Irish Parties

One important distinction between different types of consociational settlement is, as noted in Chapter 1, whether the settlement is at the regional level or not. Given that consociation emphasizes the role of elites, regional consociation emphasizes the role of *local* elites. In the eyes of critics, this is problematic as it serves to insulate the local party system, which is shaped by ethnonational division, against the progressive influence of the party system of the wider polity, which is shaped by non-ethnonational party competition and voting.

In the Northern Ireland case, integrationists claim that, in contrast to consociational institutional design, which heightens the salience of the underlying ethnonational electoral divide, a much simpler institutional change relating to the organization of political parties would significantly reduce its salience and introduce instead a more progressive dimension of political competition. Specifically, if British political parties were to run candidates in Northern Ireland elections, and fully and energetically compete in those elections, this would lead to the emergence of class-based politics, which tends to characterize British elections, at the expense of sectarian politics, which characterizes Northern Ireland elections. Integrationists seek to avoid what they see as the misguided consociational focus on "local" ethnonational parties by bringing Northern Ireland firmly into the mainstream "national" politics of the UK, with associated national (i.e., UK) non-ethnonational political debates and party competition.

This chapter empirically assesses the veracity of this argument by investigating the extent to which British (and also Irish) parties are supported by Northern Ireland citizens and, crucially, whether the determinants of such support are ethnonational in nature or class-based. The analysis should provide insight into the potential role of non-Northern Ireland parties in Northern Ireland and whether the importance of the ethnonational dimension in electoral politics in Northern Ireland is a "problem" with the supply side (the parties are ethnonational and this causes the voters to be ethnonational) or the demand side (ethnonational factors are a crucial element of electoral politics in Northern Ireland because these are the factors that ordinary people care about; changing the parties on offer won't change this). The chapter begins with an elaboration of the integrationist argument; the role of British and Irish parties in Northern Ireland party competition is then described, and the extent of, and determinants of, Northern Ireland citizens' support for British and Irish parties are investigated.

The Integrationist Argument

Roberts (1990) and Aughey (1989) argue that one of the main reasons why Northern Ireland's electoral politics has been dominated by the ethnonational question is that the main British political parties have not organized and electorally competed in Northern Ireland. Hence, political competition in Northern Ireland has been dominated by Northern Ireland-specific parties, which have prioritized conflict-related Northern Ireland-specific issues, rather than by UK-wide parties which prioritize broader socioeconomic issues relating to economic management and resource distribution. Integrationists such as Roberts and Aughey have argued that the

Northern Ireland problem of deep ethnonational division is a direct result of Northern Ireland being seen by British political parties as a distinct place with its own distinct difficulties, necessitating its own distinct party system. If British parties stopped regarding Northern Ireland as a distinct problem, it would cease to be one. Ethnonational electoral politics in Northern Ireland is not caused by the deep divisions that exist between people but rather by British parties reneging on their duty to organize and compete in Northern Ireland, abandoning Northern Ireland citizens to the limited choice of local ethnonational-obsessed parties.

Integrationists argue that there is no contradiction between unionism and frustration with the Northern Ireland unionist parties. Within unionism, the distinction between integrationists and devolutionists is described by Aughey as the difference between the idea of the union and the practice of Northern Ireland unionist organizations. The idea of unionism is consistent with full political and electoral integration with the rest of Britain and, consequently, the fully fledged operation of the Conservative party, the Labour Party, and other British parties, in Northern Ireland. Practical politics, however, means that political actors in the Northern Ireland unionist parties, and the nationalist parties also, do not wish to face electoral competition from mainland British parties. Intra-community competition is fierce enough without having to deal with the threat of leaking votes to energetically competitive "British" parties. Hence, the survivalist instincts of Northern Ireland parties prohibit a lessening of "sectarian" electoral politics.

There are, according to integrationists, unfortunate consequences for democracy of the noninvolvement of British parties in Northern Ireland elections. Northern Ireland citizens are denied the right to choose the government at Westminster elections. They cannot, as citizens would in a "normal" democracy, pass judgment on the party or parties governing the UK. Instead, their choice is restricted to Northern Ireland-specific parties who have no chance of forming a government at Westminster. Hence, there is a double negative effect of the absence of British parties: the maintenance of ethnonational electoral division and an increase in the democratic deficit.

The pro-consociation response to this argument is that electoral integration was never likely to "resolve" antagonisms in Northern Ireland. Resolution could only be facilitated by generating a power-sharing settlement between rival identity groups with long-standing antagonisms. In order to achieve such a settlement the "local" parties must be directly negotiated with, rather than wished out of existence. Hence, focusing on "local" ethnonational parties does not cause but rather is a response to, and an attempt to alleviate, long-standing deep ethnonational division. Furthermore, consociationists have argued that integrationists exaggerate the support there may be for non-Northern Ireland parties. Insofar as there is support, it may well be driven by ethnonational factors rather than "progressive" class-based factors. This is because British parties have not been neutral on the Northern Ireland conflict, and it is their positions on the conflict, rather than on any other dimension such as social class-based economic policy differences, that are likely to drive any support for them. Specifically, Labour has traditionally adopted a more pro-Catholic, pro-united Ireland position than the pro-union Conservative party and this distinction, rather than class-based factors, would determine Northern Ireland citizens' support for Labour or the Conservatives.

The integrationist argument represented an interesting suggested alternative to consociational power sharing. Since Roberts and Aughey wrote in the late 1980s, devolution has been introduced in Northern Ireland as well as Scotland and Wales, and power sharing has been established in Northern Ireland. The argument that Northern Ireland is a pseudo-democracy because the parties voters choose between cannot become decision-makers is less relevant, given that these parties run the devolved administration. However, the argument still has some relevance for UK-level government. Northern Ireland citizens did not have the option of supporting the main UK parties at the Westminster election.

The integrationist argument is interesting for current Northern Ireland politics, as it provides one suggestion for Northern Ireland making a transition, in the context of the political stability and security facilitated by the power-sharing arrangements, to a post-ethnonational politics. Could entry into the Northern Ireland political fray by British parties prompt an evolution toward postconflict politics?

And what about other sets of parties in addition to British parties? The underlying logic of the electoral integrationist argument is that political parties from country A with reputations for competing on a political dimension K could, if they traveled to, and competed in elections in, country B, in which political dimension L was highly salient, expect to be supported by citizens in country B on the basis of political dimension K rather than L. One could, in addition to focusing on the possible role of British parties in Northern Ireland, apply this counter-factual reasoning to any set of parties in the world arriving and competing in Northern Ireland. Most plausibly, the focus here is on parties from the Republic of Ireland.

Given the complex nature of the Northern Ireland conflict—a conflict between different peoples linked to different states—the negotiations leading to a settlement were international in character. The nationalists in Northern Ireland did not seek merely a power-sharing settlement within Northern Ireland in order for their interests to be protected. They also sought direct formal links between Northern Ireland and the Republic of Ireland. Hence, while the consociational power-sharing settlement is "regional" in character (a subsystem of the wider UK system), the 1998 Agreement is also international in character. In addition to power sharing within Northern Ireland, the Agreement established formal links between Northern Ireland the Republic of Ireland and also between the Republic of Ireland and Britain. The north-south links take the form of the North-South Ministerial Council, and the east-west links take the form of the British-Irish Inter-Governmental Conference.

Hence, there are firm political institutional links between Northern Ireland and the Republic of Ireland. A related question, then, is to what extent are there specifically political party-related institutional links? Are Republic of Ireland parties formally registered and organized in Northern Ireland and likely to compete in Northern Ireland elections? If so, what levels of support would they get? Crucially, for present purposes, would those determinants be ethnonational in nature or related to other factors such as social class and economic left-right beliefs? It may be seen as somewhat ironic to contemplate that people who live outside the Republic of Ireland may discern class-related differences between the Irish parties when Republic of Ireland voters have a hard job doing so (Marsh et al. 2008). Hence, our investigation of the possible class basis of Irish parties is somewhat more speculative than our investigation of British parties.

The Experience of British and Irish Parties in Northern Ireland

The British Labour party does not stand in Northern Ireland elections, an abstentionist approach that has been strongly criticized by Labour party members in Northern Ireland. Boyd Black, for example, argues: "We have our two traditional political blocs. What we need is Labour Party politics and Labour representatives, fired with Keir Hardie's passion for social justice and equality. The challenge is to bring our two communities together, and break the stranglehold of sectarianism in Northern Ireland society."[1]

Prompted by a request from Northern Ireland Labour-Party members to field candidates in local elections in Northern Ireland, the British

Labour Party National Executive Committee (NEC) decided that discussions about the merits of such a proposal should take place "with our sister parties, the Irish Labour Party (ILP) and the Social Democratic and Labour Party (SDLP)." The resulting Labour party report, leaked in January 2013, stated that both "sister" parties had grave reservations about the Labour party running candidates in Northern Ireland. The Irish Labour party's view was that if British Labour competed in Northern Ireland elections, the Irish Labour party "would face irresistible pressure to follow suit."[2] The Irish Labour party "had serious concerns about either party taking such a step" as this would be "to the detriment of the SDLP, which is already weakened by the rise of Sinn Féin." The NEC report states that Irish Labour "had grave misgivings about harming a sister party in that way." Irish Labour was also afraid of becoming inevitably embroiled in ethnonational politics if it campaigned in Northern Ireland. According to the report, Irish Labour emphasized its concern that "sectarian divisions still run deep in the North, and that both Labour and the ILP would immediately be drawn into political clashes based around those divisions, which could have political and electoral consequences outside of Northern Ireland."

For their part, representatives from the SDLP also opposed (British) Labour candidates competing in Northern Ireland, something they would view "as a hostile act which would cause a deterioration in the relationship between the SDLP and the Labour Party." Specifically, such a move by Labour would affect the strong tradition of the SDLP supporting Labour (its "sister" party) in Westminster votes. The SDLP representatives also argued that the SDLP and Labour would be competing for the same (social democratic) vote in Northern Ireland and that any decision by Labour to run would split that vote.

The report concluded that in the light of Irish Labour party and SDLP opposition to the British Labour party standing in Northern Ireland "it is the view of the NEC Review Panel that it is not advisable for the Labour party to start organising electorally in Northern Ireland." This decision was met with intense criticism from Northern Ireland Labour party members who saw the decision as "an abdication of responsible political leadership, at a time when we have a leadership void in Northern Ireland" and members were particularly derisive of the role of other parties—notably the SDLP—in apparently dictating to Labour the position it should adopt.

In contrast to Labour, the Conservatives have in recent years displayed a keenness to play an active electoral role in Northern Ireland. Up until 1972 the party was formally linked to the Ulster Unionist party, with the latter's MPs taking the Conservative party whip at Westminster. This link between the parties broke down in 1972, in the context of unionist opposition to a proposed power-sharing settlement that was part of the Sunningdale Agreement. Increasingly friendly relations between the parties in more recent times were manifested in the decision of David Trimble, former UUP leader and Northern Ireland First Minister, to take the Conservative whip in 2007 in his position in the House of Lords. The following year, UUP leader Reg Empey and Conservative party leader David Cameron set up a working group to solidify a partnership between the Conservatives and the UUP. This led to the formation of the "Ulster Conservatives and Unionists-New Force," which ran joint candidates at the 2009 and 2010 Westminster elections.

Further discussions between the parties ultimately floundered, however, as Tom Elliott, UUP leader, rejected the Conservative party's offer of a complete merger of the two parties. In the wake of this rejection by the UUP, Lord Feldman, Conservative party co-chairman, stated that "the Prime Minister has asked me to move forward in our mission to deliver mainstream, national politics to the people of Northern Ireland . . . as the Prime Minister and the Secretary of State have said, it's time to move beyond the politics of the peace process to a more normal state of affairs in which everyone can play a part in national politics."[3] Subsequently, in June 2012 the NI Conservatives were launched.

Regarding Irish parties' possible organization in Northern Ireland, Fianna Fáil has been most willing of the three main parties, with the Irish Labour Party, as noted, and Fine Gael being reluctant. Fianna Fáil declared in September 2007 that the party would begin to organize in Northern Ireland. A party committee was established to oversee the process, chaired by Dermot Ahern, minister for foreign affairs. Fianna Fáil leader and Taoiseach (prime minister) Bertie Ahern stated that "We will act gradually and strategically. We are under no illusions. It will not be easy. It will challenge us all. But I am confident we will succeed." The party established an organizational presence in the major Northern Ireland universities, and in December 2007 stated that the party had been registered in Northern Ireland by the Northern Ireland Electoral Commission. The party developed a branch (cumann) in each of the six counties in Northern Ireland, and a member from Armagh was appointed in 2009 to the party's Ard Chomhairle (national executive). Fianna Fáil activity in Northern Ireland initially prompted speculation that the party might merge with the SDLP, something firmly rejected by former leaders Seamus Mallon and Margaret Ritchie. Further development of a membership base in Northern Ireland led to Fianna Fáil declaring in 2014 its intention to compete in Northern Ireland elections from 2019 onward.

Support for British and Irish Parties

Duffy and Evans (1996) empirically examined the potential support that the British Conservative and Labour parties have in Northern Ireland, examining the extent of support and whether, in line with integrationist beliefs, such support would be motivated by non-ethnonational factors, specifically social class. Duffy and Evans used data from 1989–1991 surveys, which asked respondents to indicate whether they would vote for any of the British parties if it were possible to do so. When Duffy and Evans analyzed overlaps in the support for Northern Ireland parties and the two British parties, they found that Sinn Féin support would be the least affected by Labour and Conservative competition. In contrast, the SDLP would likely lose one-fifth of its supporters, typically to the Labour party. Unionist parties' support would be reduced, due to losing votes to the Conservative party. Alliance would be the party most affected as it would lose one third of its support to the British parties.

In terms of explaining Northern Ireland citizens' support for the British parties, Duffy and Evans find strong religious determinants: Catholics strongly prefer Labour to the Conservatives, and the reverse is true for Protestants. Duffy and Evans conclude from their extensive empirical investigation that there was "little support for the institutionalist argument that electoral integration would generate competing lines of political cleavage and thereby encourage a resolution of the Northern Irish conflict . . . the potential of British parties to bridge the communal gap is nowhere near as strong as integrationists suggest" (1996: 137).

Furthermore, Duffy and Evans find that conflict-based politics in Northern Ireland may actually be buttressed by the electoral competition of the Conservatives and Labour, because, insofar as Northern Ireland citizens would desert a Northern Ireland party in favor of a British party, it the bi-confessional Alliance party is most at risk of losing voters. Hence, a fully integrated electoral system "might bring the opposite of what many argue: a reinforcing of the ethnic cleavage through the erosion of the middle ground and the weakening of the only real political bridge across the divide that currently exists" (1996: 137).

Here, I use data from 2009 to reassess the potential impact of electoral integration. Respondents were asked to indicate the extent to which they were likely ever to vote for each of the British parties and each of the Irish parties, on a scale of 1 (would never vote for the party) to 10 (would definitely vote for the party). For simplicity, the proportion of respondents indicating between 6 and 10 on this scale are identified as being positively disposed to support the party (see Table 3.1). The Conservative party attracts almost one fifth of respondents by this measure while the British Labour party and the Liberal Democrats attract equal levels of support at 12 percent. All three Irish parties do less well, attracting between 6 and 7 percent.

Table 3.2 assesses the extent to which British and Irish party support is related to religion. The key distinction to note is that between the British Labour party and all other parties. British Labour attracts approximately equal levels of support from different religions, although tending to do better among Catholics than Protestants. The difference is not statistically significant, whereas statistically significant relations emerge in the other five party cases (indicated by * in the following tables). The British Conservatives perform particularly well among Protestants, attracting almost one in three, compared to only one in 20 Catholics.

Stark differences emerge regarding the Irish parties. Fewer than 3 percent of Protestants are positively disposed to any Irish party, while between 13 and 16 percent of Catholics are. People of other religions or of no

Table 3.1. Level of Support for British and Irish Parties

	% support
British Labour Party	12
British Conservative Party	19
British Liberal Democratic Party	12
Irish Fianna Fail Party	7
Irish Fine Gael Party	6
Irish Labour Party	7

% support = % of all respondents indicating between 6 and 10 on 1–10 "likelihood to vote" scale.

Table 3.2. Religion by Support for British and Irish Parties

	Protestants	Catholics	None	Other
British Labour	10	15	15	8
British Conservatives*	31	5	19	10
British Lib Dems*	14	8	20	11
Irish Fianna Fail*	1	16	3	3
Irish Fine Gael*	2	14	3	4
Irish Labour*	3	13	4	3

religion are similarly ill disposed to the Irish parties, and people of no religion have noticeably high levels of support for the Liberal Democrats.

Table 3.3 shows the relationship between party support and important aspects of ethnonational factors—namely, national identity, constitutional preferences, and ideological self-description. The British Labour party attracts almost identical levels of support across the different national identity groups: between 11 and 14 percent of those who describe themselves as "British," "Irish," or "Northern Irish" support British Labour. Similarly, the party attracts almost identical proportions from the constitutional-preference groups ("direct rule," "devolution/ Assembly," and "united Ireland") and the ideological groups ("unionist," "nationalist," "neither"). This consistent pattern strongly suggests that Labour can attract approximately equal levels of support across religious backgrounds and across ethnonational beliefs.

The situation for the Conservatives is markedly different. It attracts eight times more support among British than Irish respondents, six times more support among direct-rule than united-Ireland respondents, and almost 20 times more support among "unionists" than "nationalists." The position of the Liberal Democrats is somewhat slanted to unionist rather than nationalist but is much more evenly divided than that of the Conservatives.

Table 3.3. Ethnonational Beliefs and Support for British and Irish Parties

National identity

	British	Irish	Northern Irish	Other
British Labour	11	12	14	14
British Conservatives*	31	4	20	8
British Lib Dems*	13	7	14	18
Irish Fianna Fail*	1	16	6	6
Irish Fine Gael*	2	15	4	6
Irish Labour*	3	12	6	10

Constitutional preferences

	Direct rule	Assembly devolved	United Ireland
British Labour	13	11	14
British Conservatives*	31	20	5
British Lib Dems	15	12	9
Irish Fianna Fail*	2	4	22
Irish Fine Gael*	2	4	18
Irish Labour*	3	5	16

Ideological self-description

	Unionist	Neither	Nationalist
British Labour	10	13	13
British Conservatives*	38	14	2
British Lib Dems*	15	12	7
Irish Fianna Fail*	2	5	18
Irish Fine Gael*	2	4	17
Irish Labour*	3	5	14

The relationship between Northern Ireland party support and potential support for the British and Irish parties is explored in Table 3.4. The table shows the extent to which first- preference voters in the 2009 Northern Ireland EP election have positive electoral views of the British and Irish parties. This illustrates the extent to which a Northern Ireland party may be in competition with British or Irish parties and might potentially lose voters to that party if that party were to energetically organize and campaign.

Table 3.4. Northern Ireland Party Choice in 2009 European Parliament Election and Support for British and Irish Parties

	All	DUP	SDLP	SF	UUP	TUV	did not vote
British Labour*	29	14	33	11	13	10	7
British Conservatives*	31	40	8	3	56	42	12
British Lib Dems*	29	20	18	2	22	15	8
Irish Fianna Fail*	3	4	19	19	4	0	5
Irish Fine Gael*	9	4	17	13	4	0	5
Irish Labour*	11	6	24	8	5	3	5

Almost one-third of Alliance voters support each of the three British parties. Two-fifths of DUP and TUV supporters support the Conservative party and almost three-fifths of UUP voters do. All three unionist parties prefer the Liberal Democrats to the British Labour party. There is almost no support among Sinn Féin voters for either the Conservatives or the Liberal Democrats and some slight support (11 percent) for the British Labour party. In contrast the SDLP voters have much higher levels of support for the British parties; one third support Labour, one fifth support the Liberal Democrats, and 8 percent support the Conservatives. Thus, there is more difference between the two nationalist parties than between the three Conservative-supporting unionist parties.

The three unionist parties are similar in their antipathy to Irish parties. One-fifth of SDLP and Sinn Féin voters support Fianna Fáil, but the SDLP's favored Irish party is the Irish Labour party, which Sinn Féin supporters are much more lukewarm about. Alliance voters have higher levels of support for Fine Gael and Labour. Northern Ireland citizens who abstained in the 2009 election have low levels of support for any of the British and Irish parties, suggesting an antipathy to parties in general.

Would social class and economic left-right ideological difference help explain attitudes of Northern Ireland citizens to British and Irish parties?

Table 3.5. Social Class and Support for British and
Irish Parties

	AB	C1	C2	DE
British Labour	14	15	10	10
British Conservatives*	20	26	21	10
British Lib Dems*	15	18	10	6
Irish Fianna Fail	9	9	6	5
Irish Fine Gael	10	8	5	5
Irish Labour	10	7	6	6

Table 3.5 reports the relationship between social class and support. Very little difference emerges in relation to British Labour, who attract roughly equal proportions of middle-class and working-class groups. In contrast, the British Conservatives and Liberal Democrats attract greater support among the wealthier social class categories (labeled as the "AB" and "C1" social groups by some researchers and market research companies) than among the least well off (the "DE" social group). Very little difference emerges in relation to support for the Irish parties.

When economic left-right ideological views are related to party support, British Labour performs well among the most left-wing group, attracting one-fifth of that group, in contrast to only one-tenth of the centrist and right-wing groups (see Table 3.6). A similar pattern emerges for the Liberal Democrats. In contrast, support for the Conservatives is roughly equal across the economic left-right categories. The results for the Irish parties are intriguing and suggest some economic ideological basis to party support: Fianna Fáil perform better among the right-wing than the left-wing category, while the reverse is the case for the Irish Labour party.

A more complex analysis is now performed in order to identify the extent to which combinations of explanatory factors explain variation in

Table 3.6. Attitudes to Taxation/Spending and Support for British and Irish Parties

	Cut taxes + spending	Stay the same	Increase taxes + spending
British Labour*	11	9	21
British Conservatives	17	18	23
British Lib Dems*	8	10	19
Irish Fianna Fail*	12	5	8
Irish Fine Gael	8	5	8
Irish Labour*	7	4	13

the likelihood of supporting British and Irish parties. Specifically, it would be useful to identify the explanatory power of all of the "ethnonational" factors (i.e., religion and views on identity, constitutional future, and ideological identification). Also, do factors relating to social class and economic left-right ideology, when added to ethnonational and party factors, provide additional explanatory power?

Figure 3.1 shows the extent to which ethnonational, party, and social class and economic left-right ideological factors explain Northern Ireland citizens' support for British parties. The stark contrast in the graph relating to the Conservatives', compared to the Labour and Liberal Democrats', graphs is revealing. Knowing what religion people are and what their ethnonational views are is of almost no help in terms of understanding whether they are supportive of the British Labour party. Equally, such knowledge would be of little help in predicting whether someone is supportive of the Liberal Democrats. However, knowing what religion somebody is explains 16 percent of variation in whether someone supports the Conservatives, and a combination of religion and ethnonational views explains 23 percent of variation. Knowing Northern Irish party support or abstention adds predictive power to all three parties, largely a result of the impact of abstention on disinclination to support each of the

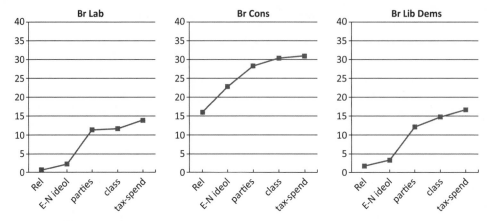

Figure 3.1. Support for British parties; increase in variation explained resulting from addition of explanatory variables.

parties. Very little added explanatory power is provided by social class and economic left-right views for Labour (neither variable is statistically significant) or the Conservatives (although social-class group is a statistically significant predictor).

The role played by class and economic values for Liberal Democrats is noteworthy, in that middle-class groups are statistically significantly more likely than the lowest social class group to support the Liberal Democrats; having left-wing rather than right-wing economic views is also a predictor. Hence, there is some support for the Liberal Democrats "crossing the divide": ethnonational factors do not strongly predict their support base, and middle-class left-oriented Northern Ireland citizens tend to support them. In short, how Northern Ireland citizens view the Conservative party is different from the way they view either Labour or the Liberal Democrats. The latter two parties potentially garner support roughly equally across the ethnonational divide, while attitudes to the Conservatives map very much onto the Northern Ireland ethnonational

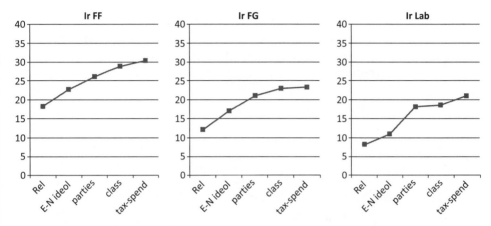

Figure 3.2. Support for Irish parties; increase in variation explained resulting from addition of explanatory variables.

divide. Although both Labour and the Liberal Democrats potentially attract voters from across the divide, only in relation to the Liberal Democrats is there any evidence of class-based voting.

In relation to the Irish parties (see Figure 3.2), the differences between the parties are less striking. However, the key difference is between Fianna Fáil and Irish Labour. Knowing what religion a Northern Ireland citizen is helps explain whether that person would support Fianna Fáil or not twice as much as that for Irish Labour. Also, knowing the religion and ethnonational views helps explain almost 25 percent of variance regarding Fianna Fáil, but just over 10 percent of the variance regarding Irish Labour. Thus, Irish Fianna Fáil and British Conservatives play a similar role: whether or not you support them depends very much on your ethnonational traits. Also, neither Irish Labour nor Irish Fine Gael can play the role British Labour and the British Liberal Democrats can play, which is to attract votes from across the community divide.

In the multivariate analysis of Irish party support it is only in relation to Fianna Fáil that class and economic values are, controlling for all other ethnonational and partisan factors, statistically significant. Middle-class respondents with right-wing economic views tended to support Fianna Fáil.

Conclusion

The findings are extremely similar to previous findings from the late 1980s and early 1990s. Labour and the Conservatives are viewed very differently by the two communities. Catholics, Irish identifiers, nationalists, and pro-united-Irelanders are much more favorably disposed to the Labour party than to the Conservative party and the reverse is true for Protestants, British identifiers, unionists, and direct rule supporters. However, this difference between Labour and the Conservatives should not mask the fact that one of these parties—Labour—attracts support fairly evenly across both communities. In that sense, integrationists are correct in their thinking that there is potential for British parties to attract support across the divide. However, of the two main parties it is Labour who refuse to organize in Northern Ireland, rather than the Conservatives, who are very keen to do so, who can perform that task. Hence, integrationists might valuably argue not for British parties per se but rather simply for the Labour party. There are two drawbacks however, from the integrationist perspective. First, the price of Labour activism would, as the SDLP are highly aware, be a decline of the SDLP, as the support bases of these two parties overlap considerably. Also, the Alliance party would suffer, but Alliance would suffer almost equally from the activism of any of the three British parties. Hence, it is parties widely perceived as moderate or neutral on the ethnonational issue who would suffer electorally.

The Liberal Democrats are interesting in that they do fairly equally well across the ethnic blocs and have an identifiable basis to their support in terms of social class and economic ideology. Controlling for ethnic factors, middle-class left-wingers in Northern Ireland are supportive of the Liberal Democrats. However, Liberal Democrat support would likely come at a cost to the party with which this support most closely overlaps—Alliance.

Chapter 4

Electoral Accountability
and Performance-Based Voting

The previous two chapters have investigated the ideological basis of voting behavior. This chapter and the next take a different approach. Rather than focusing on the opposing positions citizens may adopt (for example, pro- versus anti-united Ireland, or economic left-wing versus right-wing) and how these stances drive vote choice, the focus is on how citizens evaluate the ability of each of the parties to perform particular functions.

In the international literature on democracy and elections, performance-based voting is assumed to be a crucial ingredient of democratic accountability. The most straightforward model of citizens holding governments to account via performance-based voting assumes a two-party system, with one governing party and one opposition party, very clear lines of responsibility (the government is responsible for life getting better or worse), and reward/punishment-based voting behavior (voters support the government if they think life has gotten better, but support the opposition party if they think life has gotten worse) (Key 1966; Fiorina 1981). This clear picture of democratic accountability in action is, however, blurred by a number of institutional factors (Powell and Whitten 1993; Hobolt, Tilley, and Banducci 2013). For example, multilevel government can lead to a lack of clarity about what exactly the national-level government, as opposed to a sub- or supranational level of government, is responsible for (Johns 2011; Cutler 2004, 2008). Also, coalition governments in multiparty systems undermine the simple government-opposition dichotomy and beg the question which particular governing party should be punished if life has gotten worse, and which particular opposition party should be rewarded (Anderson 2000; Duch and Stevenson 2008; Fisher and Hobolt 2010).

Most governments are coalition governments (Hobolt and Karp 2010), and most of these operate, to varying degrees of significance, in a multilevel government context (Hooghe and Marks 2001; Hooghe, Marks, and Schakel 2010). Thus, citizens in many countries are faced with the vertical (multilevel government) and horizontal (coalition government) blurring of the lines of political responsibility and must confront the very daunting challenge of identifying which particular political actor should be held to account at election time.

In the regional and all-inclusive consociational power-sharing context of Northern Ireland 2007–2011, these vertical and horizontal constraints on responsibility attribution are especially acute, potentially posing serious problems for the operation of political accountability and casting doubt on the democratic nature of the Northern Ireland political institutional arrangements. This may be seen as a specific example of the general and frequently voiced criticism of consociational arrangements: they are undemocratic because they do not allow the voters to hold the government to account. Inclusive power sharing, it is argued, leaves little or no room for meaningful opposition, and no clear mechanism for replacing a "bad" government with an alternative government (Brass 1991: 334–39; Jung and Shapiro 1995; see discussion in O'Leary 2005). Electoral accountability in the case of an all-inclusive coalition government, with associated difficulties in terms of identifying where responsibility lies in the large multiparty government and identifying an alternative government, may be thought of as the extreme case of a general phenomenon: electoral accountability in the coalition context. In addition to the all-inclusive nature of the 2007–2011 Northern Ireland power-sharing coalition, the Northern Ireland case presents a further challenge to responsibility attribution, given its status as a "regional" consociation; a devolved power-sharing administration operating in the context of the larger UK polity. Under the 1998 Agreement that established devolution and power sharing, Northern Ireland's Assembly became the third aspect of regional decision making in the UK, along with the Welsh and Scottish Assemblies established after the 1997 referendums. Given that the Assembly operated sporadically up to 2002 and was suspended during the 2002–2007 period, the 2007–2011 government was the first inclusive functioning power-sharing government that citizens, at the 2011 Assembly election, were asked to pass judgment on. This chapter focuses on voter choice at the 2011 election and seeks to identify whether there is any evidence of performance-based (i.e., accountability-based) voting. Two possible ways in which electoral accountability may operate in the Northern Ireland consociational context are examined.

The first approach makes quite limited assumptions about citizens' ability to engage in responsibility attribution and performance-based voting. This model assumes that citizens assess the overall performance of the power-sharing government and distinguish between strongly influential and weakly influential governing parties (perhaps on the basis of which parties hold the co-prime minister positions or the relative number of cabinet seats the parties hold. The parties perceived as powerful in the coalition are rewarded by voters if the government performed well and are punished if the government performed badly. Parties that are not perceived to be powerful in the coalition are not judged on the basis of government performance, because they did not do much to influence that performance. Accordingly, in each community bloc, citizens' choice between the two main governing parties is assumed to be driven by overall evaluation of the performance of the power-sharing government, conditional on the attribution of relative responsibility for governing performance to the two governing parties.

The second approach makes much more onerous demands on voters. This model assumes that citizens attribute responsibility—across a range of issue areas—to the appropriate level of government and to specific governing parties. The model assumes that voters reflecting on the performance of the power-sharing government must ask the following questions. In relation to a particular issue domain (such as the economy, health services, the maintenance of peace, and so on), has life gotten better or worse? Was the devolved power-sharing government actually responsible for this? If it was responsible, which particular governing party in the power-sharing executive, if any, was most responsible? Performance-based electoral accountability may then operate if responsibility, for this issue domain, is attributed not only to the power-sharing government but also to a specific governing party, and voters reward or punish the party accordingly.

Simple Model: Overall Evaluation and Accountability

Much of the previous work on performance-based voting in the coalition context has focused on demonstrating that performance models work less well in the coalition context than in the single- party context, given the higher clarity of responsibility in the single-party- government context and the difficulty for citizens in identifying who the responsible actors are in a complicated multiparty government context (Lewis-Beck 1988; Paldam 1991; Fisher and Hobolt 2010). Further research has tried to distinguish between different types of coalitions rather than simply comparing coalition government to single-party government. "Complex" coalitions are those which include many rather than few parties and in which power is quite dispersed rather than concentrated in one dominant coalition party. The more complex, or less "cohesive," the coalition, the less likely performance-based voting is (Lewis Beck 1988; Anderson 2000; Duch and Stevenson 2008; Hobolt, Tilley, and Banducci 2013.

Very few previous studies have addressed the question as to whether the different parties in a coalition government are assessed differently by voters. Anderson (2000) and Duch and Stevenson (2008) suggest that some coalition parties are obviously more influential than others, and voters are more likely to hold the powerful governing coalition parties to account, via retrospective economic voting, than the nonpowerful coalition parties. Two institutional factors in particular are likely to signal to voters which parties are particularly important: the party that holds the prime ministership, and parties that hold relatively large numbers of cabinet portfolios (Anderson 2000; Duch and Stevenson 2008). Fisher and Hobolt (2010) focus on citizens' overall evaluation of government performance, rather than narrowly focusing on the economic-issue domain, and find that retrospective performance-based voting is indeed stronger for those coalition parties that hold the premiership, but there is no additional "party size" effect. This suggests that citizens' perceptions of the relative power of different coalition parties is driven by knowledge of which party the prime minister is from: this party is then clearly punished or rewarded depending on the performance of the government, and the other coalition parties are essentially absolved of responsibility, being neither rewarded nor punished, because of their uninfluential status in the government.

Here, in tandem with Fisher and Hobolt (2010), voters are assumed to come to an overall evaluation as to whether the Northern Ireland power-sharing government performed well or not. Voters are also assumed to identify differences in the overall level of influence that each party had in the power sharing government. From the formal positions held by the governing parties, voters may have inferred that Sinn Féin and the

DUP were particularly influential, given that they held the positions of first minister and deputy first minister, formally equal co-prime minister positions. Also, Sinn Féin and the DUP were the two largest parties in terms of Cabinet seats (as well as first preference votes and parliamentary seats), holding between 31 and 38 percent of the positions, the other three parties in government holding only one or two Cabinet seats each (see Figure 4.1).

In order to assess how citizens perceived the relative importance of the five governing parties, respondents in the 2011 post-election survey were asked:

> Taking each party in turn, how much importance or influence do you think it had in the 2007–2011 power-sharing government: a lot of influence, some influence, not much influence, no influence at all [each of the five parties asked separately].

The survey evidence suggests that voters were clearly able to identify differences in the relative overall influence of the parties. Between 63 and 65 percent of all voters stated that Sinn Féin and the DUP had "a lot of influence," compared to only between 6 and 8 percent who stated that the SDLP, UUP, or Alliance had "a lot of influence."

Respondents were also asked how well they thought the power-sharing government had performed in the 2007–2011 period:

> How satisfied are you with the performance of the Northern Ireland power-sharing government between 2007–2011: very satisfied, fairly satisfied, not very satisfied, not satisfied at all?

The response to this question is reported in Figure 4.3, and it emerges that overall evaluations are positive. Over 70 percent indicated that they

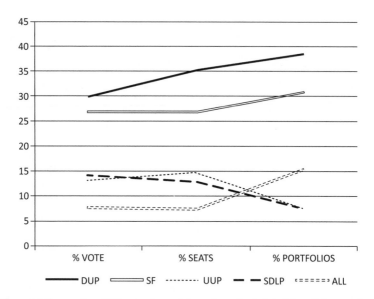

Figure 4.1. Proportion 2011 vote, Assembly seats and ministerial positions each party holds.

were very or fairly satisfied, although the vast majority were fairly rather than very satisfied. There was some difference by religion, with Catholics somewhat more satisfied than Protestants (13 percent of Protestants were "not at all satisfied" compared to 6 percent of Catholics).

In order to test the "simple" model of performance-based voting, variables are first of all created which represent citizens' assessment of the relative influence of the two governing parties in each bloc. Appendix Table A2 reports the results of a binary logistic regression which seeks to assess whether evaluation of the performance of the government predicts unionist vote choice (i.e., choice between the UUP and DUP), conditional on perceived relative influence of the DUP and UUP (with appropriate control variables included). The interaction between the evaluation variable and the perceived relative influence variable is statistically

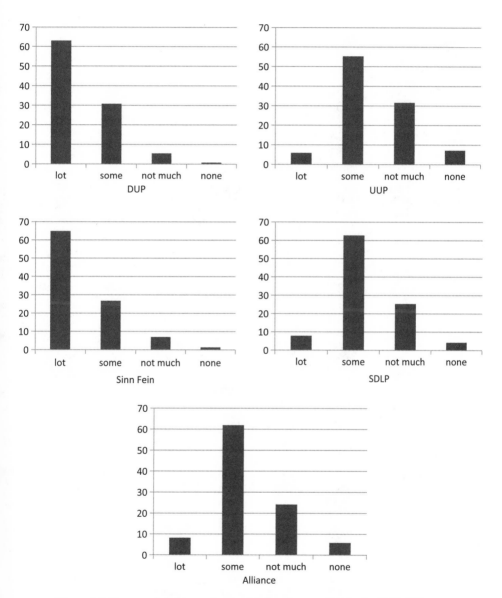

Figure 4.2. How much influence do you think each party had in the 2007–2011 power sharing government? All voters.

all voters

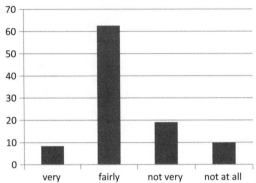

Protestant voters

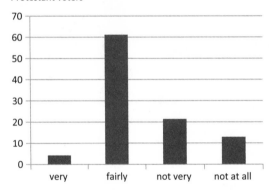

Catholic voters

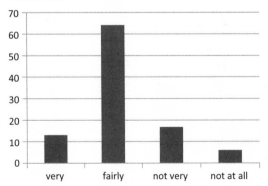

Figure 4.3. How satisfied are you with the performance of the power sharing government 2007–2011?

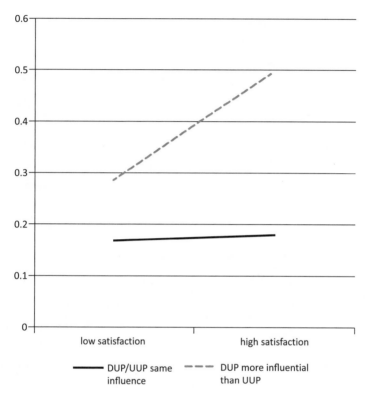

Figure 4.4. Impact on probability of voting for DUP (rather than UUP) of an increase in overall satisfaction with power-sharing government, conditional on perceived relative influence of DUP and UUP in the government. An increase in the level of satisfaction represents a one-unit shift on the 4-point satisfaction scale, from 2 (not very satisfied) to 3 (fairly satisfied); "DUP more influential" represents a two-unit move on the "relative influence" scale, from 0 (both parties of same influence) to 2 (DUP 2 units higher influence than UUP).

significant, and the magnitude of the effect is graphically illustrated in Figure 4.4. Essentially, satisfaction with the performance of the government predicts support for the DUP for those voters who perceive the DUP to be more influential than the UUP (the steep line in the graph), but there is no relationship between satisfaction and vote choice for those voters who see the two parties as equally responsible (the flat line in the graph). A similar model (Model 2 in Appendix Table A2) was conducted for vote choice in the nationalist bloc (i.e., choice between Sinn Féin and the SDLP), but no statistically significant conditioning effect emerged.

Complex Model: Issue-Specific Accountability

This model assumes a more sophisticated engagement by voters with the issue of responsibility attribution. Voters are assumed to make assessments as to whether things have gotten better or worse across a range of issue domains, rather than focusing either on one, such as the economy, or on an overall evaluation. Voters are also assumed to identify, in relation to each issue domain, whether the government was actually responsible and, if it was responsible, which governing party—if any—was particularly responsible.

Previous research internationally has assessed the extent to which appropriate attribution of responsibility across different levels of government conditions vote choice. For example, in an analysis of electoral accountability in the context of Canadian federalism, Cutler (2008) compared citizens' attributions of responsibility across the provincial and federal levels to experts' attributions. Cutler finds that citizens are not very accurate in their responsibility attributions, although "better educated and more attentive citizens get substantially closer to the expert judgement" (2008: 645). In another analysis that links responsibility attribution to vote choice, Cutler (2004) suggests that multilevel government undermines electoral accountability, finding that voters are unlikely to rely on issue areas that are ambiguous in terms of assignment of responsibility. Johns (2011) investigated citizens' perceptions of who is responsible in the Scottish/UK and Ontario/Canada cases and concluded that, insofar as attributions are accurate, they are not actually relied on in terms of shaping vote choice: "when called upon in surveys to do so, many voters can confidently and fairly accurately assign issues to different levels of government. Yet they do not seem to consider these attributions much at elections. There is little indication that issues weighed heavier in the decision making of those who regarded them as the responsibility of that arena" (53).

More positively, Arceneaux concludes that there is some evidence of responsibility attribution conditioning vote choice, but only under certain conditions: "citizens do make distinctions among levels of government when evaluating issues, but they only link these distinctions to their voting decisions if those issue attitudes are highly accessible" (2006: 731).

These mixed findings suggest that multilevel government does lead to some confusion for voters in terms of attributing responsibility and holding government to account. How widespread are such difficulties in the Northern Ireland case? To what extent do voters hold the devolved power-sharing executive responsible, and how does this vary across issue areas? One might, for example, imagine that there would be relatively few voters believing the government was mainly responsible for the Northern Ireland economy, given the limited economic power devolved and the high level of dependence on the central UK government, as well as the highly globalized nature of economic developments in any case (see discussion in Keating 2007). In contrast, one might perhaps expect a widespread perception of Northern Ireland government responsibility for education, given the high and consistent level of controversy associated with the executive's approach to education policy in the 2007–2011 period (Matthews 2012: 356).

In addition to the challenge of deciding whether a particular level of government is responsible for a particular issue area, there is the further challenge of deciphering—in the event of a coalition government—which particular governing party, if any, was especially responsible for that issue area. There are perhaps three types of issues where accountability matters in a post-conflict setting such as Northern Ireland. First, there are what are sometimes called "normal" or "bread and butter" policy domains, for example, health, social services, and general economic performance (employment and growth), which are important in most democracies. Second, there are conflict areas relating to policing, security, and political stability, and to consociational autonomy (e.g., primary and secondary education and symbolic issues, including language, politics). Third, there are conflict areas relating to group representation (Mitchell, Evans, and O'Leary 2009).

In terms of trying to investigate how the different parties within a coalition may be differently assessed by voters across different issue domains, it is suggested here that two "signals" to voters may be especially important in terms of attributing responsibility. First, which particular ministerial offices the parties hold in the coalition may be important in terms of indicating where responsibility may lie across the different governing parties. For example, citizens' evaluations of the performance of the health services may be a stronger predictor of voting for the party holding the ministerial responsibility for health than for other parties. Similarly, the party in charge of education might be more likely than other parties to be judged on the basis of evaluations of the quality of education provision (and similarly for defense, environment, and so on). The importance of different ministries underlies one of the most influential explanations of coalition formation. Laver and Shepsle's (1998) model of multiparty government formation is based on the premise that parties bargain over controlling distinct issue areas via the institutional mechanism of (non-prime ministerial) ministerial portfolio allocation (on ministerial autonomy; see Laver and Shepsle 1994). One might plausibly expect that the ministries that parties are responsible for would, in addition to being important for elite bargaining, also be important for voters in terms of acting as a cue as to which party to hold responsible for a particular policy domain. In the Northern Ireland context, and as noted in previous chapters, portfolio allocation is an inherent part of government formation. Portfolios are chosen by parties in line with a divisor method of portfolio distribution—specifically the d'Hondt formula (on the application of this mechanism see O'Leary, Grofman, and Elklit 2005; McEvoy 2006). Portfolios are chosen sequentially, and turn taking is ordered by party size (in terms of the number of Assembly seats). Specific portfolios relevant to the analysis in this chapter include the Finance ministry (held by the DUP), the Health ministry (held by the UUP), and the Education ministry (held by Sinn Féin).

In addition to the institutional signal to voters relating to which party holds which specific portfolios, a second possible signal relates to party reputations. For instance, some parties may base their support on protecting particular sectional interests (farmers, business people, and so on), and parties may be judged in terms of how good a job they were perceived to have done in terms of protecting "their" sector. Or parties may simply prioritize certain issue areas (e.g., the environment) and may be evaluated by citizens on those particular areas. (On parties' emphasis on particular issue domains and interests see Budge and Farlie 1983; Petrocik 1996.) In Northern Ireland, one of the most important issues on which parties hold reputations relates to the competency with which they can represent their respective community's interests in decision making in the power-sharing executive. Specifically, and as noted earlier, the DUP is widely held to be the main party robustly representing the interests of Protestants, and Sinn Féin is viewed as the main party robustly defending the interests of Catholics (see discussion in Mitchell, Evans, and O'Leary 2009).

Hence, via either institutional factors (portfolio holding) or reputational factors (issue ownership), a clarity of party profile may indicate to citizens a clarity of party responsibility. Citizens may be influenced by these, or other, cues and come to a conclusion as to which parties are responsible for what issue areas. Furthermore, citizens may rely on this information regarding responsibility attribution when they engage in performance-based voting. The expectation, then, may be stated as follows: party choice in the regional and all-inclusive consociational context is driven by citizens' evaluations of aspects of life conditional on citizens' attribution of responsibility, first to the regional power-sharing government, and second to specific governing parties, for these aspects of life.

In order to empirically test this expectation, respondents were asked to evaluate whether certain aspects of life in Northern Ireland had gotten better or worse. These included "the economy," "the education system," "the health service," "policing and justice," "peace, security, and political stability," "the lives of Protestants," and "the lives of Catholics." For each aspect of life, respondents were asked whether it was the responsibility of the Northern Ireland government or not. If the respondent indicated that the government was responsible, the respondent was then asked whether any particular party (or parties) was responsible. As an example, the battery relating to the economy is below:

> Thinking back over the last four years—the lifetime of the 2007 to 2011 power-sharing government—would you say that the economy in Northern Ireland over that period of time: got a lot better, got a little better, stayed the same, got a little worse, got a lot worse.

Was this:

Mainly due to the policies of the Northern Ireland government

Mainly due to other factors

Which particular political party, or parties, in the Northern Ireland government do you think was most responsible for influencing how the economy performed in Northern Ireland?

Variation in the extent to which respondents perceived that things had gotten better or worse on these issue areas is reported in Figure 4.5. This shows that voters believed that life had gotten worse rather than better in regard to the economy, education, and health. The balance of evaluation was strongly negative in each case (between −46 and −50). There were much more positive evaluations regarding policing and justice, and peace, security, and stability (overall balance of evaluations between +33 and +45). Stark differences emerge regarding how voters assess the lives of Protestants and the lives of Catholics. Only slightly more people had thought Protestants' lives had gotten better rather than worse. In contrast, it was widely perceived that the lives of Catholics had improved (balance of +42 compared to +6 for Protestants).

These figures relate to the assessments of voters as a whole, and there are some interesting differences when the figures are broken down by community. Catholics are less likely than Protestants to be negative about the economy and education, and Catholics are more likely than Protestants to be positive about peace, security, and stability. There is very little difference in how Catholics and Protestants evaluate the lives of Catholics in the 2007–2011 period, but Protestants are more likely than Catholics to have negative evaluations of how the lives of Protestants fared in this period.

Voters' attributions of responsibility to government and to specific parties for these issue areas, as well as a summary measure of evaluations,

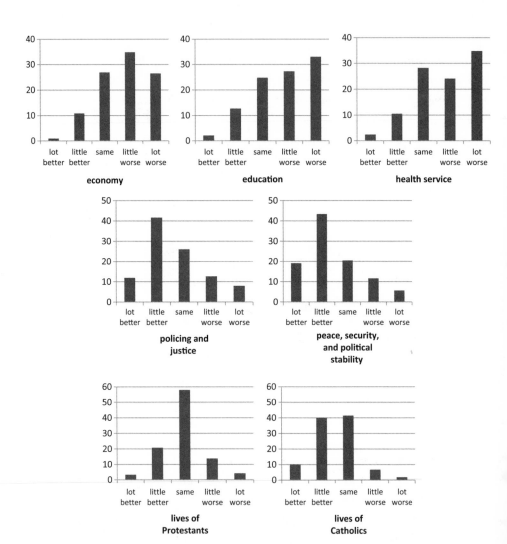

Figure 4.5. Over the 2007–2011 period did things get better or worse? All voters.

Table 4.1. Evaluations and Attributions to Government and to Party

| | Balance of attribute evaluation to NI govt. | | Attribute to party (% of all voters) | | | | |
			DUP	SDLP	SF	UUP	All
Economy	−50.0	30.7	<u>6.3</u>	1.2	5.8	1.2	0.6
Education	−45.5	57.9	7.1	2.5	<u>32.5</u>	2.8	2.3
Health	−46.0	44.5	7.6	1.7	4.9	<u>6.0</u>	0.9
Policing and Justice	+33.0	50.4	10.6	2.2	14.1	1.7	<u>2.2</u>
Peace, Security and Stability	+45.2	44.5	11.5	3.1	11.9	2.5	2.3
Interests of Protestants	+6.0	32.0	<u>15.4</u>	0.7	4.1	3.6	0.6
Interests of Catholics	+41.8	34.9	4.5	3.9	<u>19.7</u>	0.4	0.9
Average			9.0	2.2	13.3	2.6	1.4

Voters only; "balance of evaluation" for a given issue area is the percentage indicating that things got better (a lot or a little) minus the percentage indicating that things got worse (a lot or a little); parties holding the associated specific ministerial portfolios underlined; parties with strong reputations regarding the interests of each community also underlined.

are reported in Table 4.1. Less than one-third of voters hold the Northern Ireland government responsible for the economy, while almost three-fifths hold it responsible for the education services. Approximately half hold it responsible for health service provision, policing and justice, and peace and security, with about one-third of voters believing that it is the Northern Ireland government which is mainly responsible for affecting the lives of Catholics and the lives of Protestants. For each issue area, respondents who indicated that they held the Northern Ireland government responsible were then asked if they held any party in particular responsible. One-third of all voters hold Sinn Féin responsible for education (an issue area, as noted, for which the party held the portfolio). Also, one-fifth hold Sinn Féin responsible for the lives of Catholics (an issue area strongly emphasized by the party), and 12 to 14 percent of voters hold the party responsible for policing and justice as well as for peace, security, and stability. The other party to attract sizeable proportions of respondents assigning it responsibility is the DUP. The highest percentage (15 percent) held the party responsible for the lives of Protestants (a high-priority area for the party), with policing/justice and peace/security/stability attracting the next highest attribution rates. The SDLP and Alliance attract very few responses, as do the UUP, although 6 percent of voters assign responsibility to it for the health services (a portfolio held by the UUP). The DUP might have expected more assignment of responsibility to it for the economy, as it held that portfolio, but it was joint highest (with SF), and the figures are low, given that relatively few respondents believed the Northern Ireland government was responsible for the economy anyway.

Voters' evaluations and attributions are now related to their choice of party. Competition between the two unionist parties (DUP and UUP) is examined first. The 310 DUP/ UUP voters in the dataset are focused on, and, for each issue area, the proportion of the 310 who held either the DUP or the UUP uniquely responsible for that issue area is identified. Only in relation to one of the seven issue areas was the proportion higher than 10 percent. Specifically, 14 percent held the DUP uniquely responsible for "the lives of Protestants." In order to assess whether party support in the unionist bloc was driven by evaluations of the lives of Protestants over the 2007–2011 period conditional on the attribution of responsibility for this to the DUP, a logistic regression was conducted containing the appropriate predictors and interactions—namely, evaluation of the lives of Protestants, whether or not the DUP was attributed responsibility for this, and a variable capturing the interaction of these two variables (plus controls). The interaction of evaluations and attribution is highly statistically significant (as reported in Appendix Table A3). The magnitude of the interaction effect is graphically illustrated in Figure 4.6. It shows

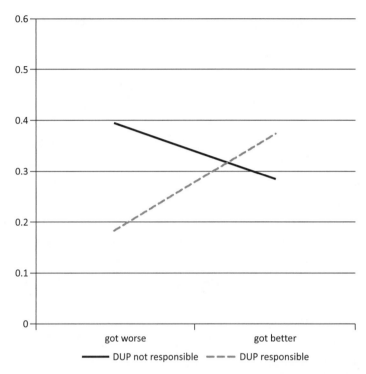

Figure 4.6. Impact on probability of voting for DUP (rather than UUP) of an increase in perception that Protestants' lives got better, conditional on attribution of responsibility to DUP. The move from "got worse" to "got better" represents a shift from half a standard deviation below the mean to half a standard deviation above the mean.

that the relationship between a positive evaluation of the lives of Protestants and the probability of voting DUP is conditional upon attribution of responsibility to the DUP. Essentially, if you think the lives of Protestants have improved and you think the DUP was responsible for this, you will vote for the DUP. If you think the lives of Protestants have gotten better but you do not attribute responsibility for this to the DUP, you will be unlikely to vote DUP.

A similar exercise was carried out in the nationalist bloc. Of the 278 SDLP/Sinn Féin voters in the dataset, over 10 percent of them uniquely attributed responsibility to Sinn Féin for four issue areas: education (25.9 percent), policing and justice (14.0 percent), peace, security, and stability (12.6 percent), and the lives of Catholics (11.5 percent). Distinct models with appropriate interaction terms included were run, but the interactions did not emerge as statistically significant in any of the models (Appendix Table A4).

Discussion

The vertical distribution and horizontal sharing of power in the multilevel multiparty government context creates a daunting challenge for citizens in terms of allocating political responsibility and holding political decision makers to account at election time. This challenge is acute in the regional and all-inclusive consociational power-sharing context, where vertical and horizontal responsibility attribution difficulties are maximized. Despite the extremely difficult context, strong evidence is found, in the unionist bloc but not the nationalist bloc, of a relatively simple model of responsibility attribution and accountability at play. Party choice of unionist voters was driven by evaluation of the overall performance of the power-sharing government, conditional on the attribution of relative influence to the different governing unionist parties (DUP and UUP). Also found was support for a more complex model of accountability at play. Issue-specific attribution of responsibility to the level of government and also to a particular party did condition the impact of issue-specific evaluations on vote choice. The support was strong in relation to the one issue tested in the unionist bloc, but no evidence emerged in the nationalist bloc. In short, electoral accountability, via attribution-sensitive retrospective performance-based voting, operates in Northern Ireland, albeit in the unionist bloc and not the nationalist bloc.

Interestingly, the results suggest an asymmetry in terms of the operation of electoral accountability: it is observable in the unionist bloc but not in the nationalist bloc. Chapter 2 also found asymmetric results—namely that ethnonational ideology plays a much stronger predictive role in the nationalist than the unionist bloc, probably due to the traditionally much greater ethnonational divergence between the (moderate constitutionalist) SDLP and (irredentist paramilitarist) Sinn Féin than ever existed between the two unionist parties. The asymmetric findings in Chapter 2 and this chapter may suggest a general phenomenon in the post-conflict consociational setting: that there is more political space for performance-based voting to operate in the particular bloc in which the ethnonational ideological conflict dimension is least salient.

Hence, this chapter finds evidence supporting the operation of electoral accountability in Northern Ireland. Like other multiparty systems operating in a multilevel government context, democratic accountability at election time is difficult, given the challenge of attributing responsibility. There may be a trade-off in any democratic system between the sharing of power, horizontally and vertically, and the ease with which political responsibility may be attributed. Given the very significant sharing of power in the Northern Ireland case, profound attribution difficulties are to be expected. Despite the difficulties, performance-based voting, and hence electoral accountability, operates, at least in the unionist bloc.

While this chapter has focused on performance-based voting in the intra-bloc context, the next chapter shifts the focus to performance-based voting in the cross-bloc context. What potential is there in Northern Ireland for citizens to vote for "rival community" parties? Insofar as there is any potential for cross-divide voting, is it shaped by perceptions of the ability of rival parties to perform important functions in the power-sharing executive? Furthermore, given that the findings so far—from Chapter 2 and from this chapter—highlight the asymmetry of party competition and voting, is potential performance-based cross-bloc voting asymmetrical also?

Chapter 5

Performance and Potentially Voting Across the Divide

The previous chapter focused on performance-based voting in the context of intra-community vote choice. Here, I focus on performance-based voting in the context of the potential for voting across the divide. In order to explain potential cross-community voting, I elaborate the concept of ethnic catch-all voting, whereby citizens' levels of support for parties from a rival ethnic bloc are a function of citizens' evaluations of the ability of such parties to represent the interests of all of the competing communities. I argue that using the concept of ethnic catch-all voting to explain potential cross-community voting complements Mitchell et al.'s use of the concept of ethnic tribune voting (discussed in Chapter 4) to explain intra-bloc vote choice (supporting the party in your own ethnic bloc that you perceive to be the best at representing your ethnic group's interests).

To identify which particular cross-bloc parties are likely to be perceived as more competent than others in terms of performing an ethnic catch-all function, I distinguish between issue-based and valence-based voting (following Stokes 1963) and theorize the link between the two, building on arguments made in Mitchell et al. (2009) and Sanders et al. (2012). I argue that valence judgments are likely to be driven by party positions. Specifically, I argue that parties that have consistently held moderate ethnonational positions will enjoy an ethnic catch-all valence advantage. In other words, if two parties in a rival bloc are currently adopt-ing moderate ethnonational positions, the party that previously adopted an extreme position will be less credible as an ethnic catch-all party than the party that did not previously adopt an extreme position: hawkish party origins militate against, while dovish party origins facilitate, posi-tive perceptions of rival bloc parties' abilities to perform the ethnic catch-all function.

Ethnic Catch-All Voting

Mitchell et al. (2009) argue that the compromises made by Sinn Féin and the DUP on constitutional and power-sharing issues have indeed led to both parties in each bloc currently occupying the moderate center-ground, irrespective of the parties' formerly extreme positions. However, what does now differentiate the parties in each bloc is how capable the parties are perceived to be of representing the interests of their community in the executive—that is, their capacity to act as ethnic tribune parties. Once all parties in a deeply divided place have agreed to share power, and have thus, essentially, accepted the legitimacy of the state, constitutional issues recede in importance and are replaced by the now crucial issue of how resources are to be allocated by the new power-sharing government. Voters assess the relative competence of each of the parties in their bloc to "deliver" for that community in the power-sharing government, and the party best placed to "perform well" in terms of representing its community's interests will be electorally rewarded (Mitchell et al. 2009).

According to Mitchell et al. (2009)—and similarly argued by Mit-chell and Evans (2009) and by McGarry and O'Leary (2009)—within-community party competition has moved away from being issue-based (i.e., relating to parties' positions, in this case on constitutional matters and power sharing) and has instead become valence-based (relating to relative evaluations of parties' reputations for efficiently performing a particular function, in this case parties representing robustly their community in resource-allocation decision making in the executive). Essentially, movement by the "extreme" parties to the center ground on constitutional issues is married to a robust reputation on community representation. It is this combination of issue moderation and valence robustness that explains the recent electoral success of the DUP and Sinn Féin.

An important aspect of Mitchell et al.'s (2009) argument is that this "combination" is also causally related, in the sense that the extent to which a party has a reputation for robustly defending the interests of the community (i.e., its "tribune" reputation) is a function of the party's former position on constitutional matters. For clarity, I sketch the Mitchell et al. (2009) description of changes in party position that underpins their "ethnic tribune party" argument (Figure 5.1). Essentially, Mitchell et al. argue that a voter in a given bloc (i.e., either a nationalist voter or a unionist voter) at time 2 is faced with parties that are close in terms of ethnonational position. Performance-based voting is likely to be important at time 2, given the rise in salience of the protection of community interests in the new power-sharing government. In order to identify which party is best able to represent their group interests, voters will take into account both past and present positions of parties on the ethnonational cleavage. Mitchell et al. (402) state that voters in a particular community seek to be "represented by their 'strongest voice.' Typically this will be parties with reputations for tough bargaining, and such reputations will partly be based on their past records of less-moderate policy positions."

Hence, a nationalist voter will reason as follows: because Sinn Féin has historically been extreme/hardline on the ethnonational dimension (as per time 1 in Figure 5.1), Sinn Féin is currently more credible as a robust defender of community interests. Similarly, a unionist voter will reason that the UUP and DUP are very similar now in terms of ethnonational

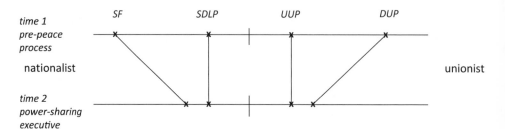

Figure 5.1. Sketch of Mitchel et al. (2009) discussion of party position.

position, but because the DUP used to have a more extreme position than the UUP it (the DUP) is best placed to staunchly defend unionist interests. In short, position drives valence—and more specifically prior ethnonational position drives current ethnic tribune valence.

The "position drives valence" argument in Mitchell et al. (2009) is consistent with the argument later elaborated by Sanders et al. (2012) in the context of British voting behavior. They find that

> spatial calculations act as a source of valence judgements. The hypothesis considered is that Downs undergirds Stokes—voters use spatial calculations as heuristic devices when assessing party competence. Parties viewed as closer than their competitors to voters in spatial terms are more likely to be judged as credible vehicles for achieving widely shared policy goals such as economic prosperity, health care and public safety. Analyses are consistent with this spatial cueing hypothesis. (312)

The interesting distinction between Mitchell et al.'s (2009) argument and Sanders et al.'s (2012) argument relates to the time point of position that performs the valence cueing. In Sanders et al. (2012), it is current positional factors that cue current valence judgments, whereas in

Mitchell et al. it is prior (historical) positional factors that cue current valence judgments.

The weak "tribune" reputations of certain parties, such as the UUP and the SDLP, should not necessarily be a disadvantage for the parties in the medium term. This is because the UUP and SDLP moderate positions, historically and currently, can leave them well placed in terms of non-tribune-type representation—namely, what is here termed ethnic catch-all representation. This is the reputation for being able, at least to some significant extent, to represent both of the competing communities; or, to put it slightly differently, to represent the other community in addition to representing their own community. The consistently nonextreme positions, over time, of the UUP and the SDLP on constitutional matters (as sketched in Figure 5.1) arguably give them reputational credibility in terms of an ethnic catch-all function.

Using the term "ethnic catch-all" to describe a party is an attempt to convey the idea of a party broadening its appeal beyond the demographic/ethnic group that it initially attracted support from. Kirchheimer (1966) described as "catch-all" those socialist parties who sought to broaden their appeal beyond the boundaries of the working class. A catch-all party seeks to reduce the priority placed on ideology and narrow social groups and instead seeks to appeal increasingly to a broader range of citizens (Wolinetz 2002).

In their examination of party modernization in deeply divided places, Gormley-Heenan and MacGinty (2008) discuss the possibility of parties broadening their electoral appeal. The authors focus on the illustrative case of the DUP and, in a similar vein to Mitchell et al.'s (2009) argument, suggest that the DUP has moved from being a staunchly and comprehensively hardline (premodern or nonmodern) party to a party which subtly combines elements of intransigence with elements of progressiveness/modernism. As well as increased centralization, professionalization, engagement with the state, and employment of technologically advanced election campaigning, Gormley-Heenan and MacGinty discuss broadening of electoral appeal within the Protestant community as a fifth facet of DUP party modernization: "Clearly, in the context of divided societies, the likelihood of a 'classic' catch-all party prospering is remote. . . . In order to maximise support in ethnic elections, parties must reflect societal fissures and garner support *in their own bloc*" (2008: 56, emphasis added). Gormley-Heenan and MacGinty argue that the DUP, for example, has attempted to broaden its electoral base by appealing to both the fundamentalist wing associated with Ian Paisley and, increasingly, to the more secular wing of Protestants associated with, for example, Peter Robinson.

Given Gormley-Heenan and MacGinty's focus on the DUP up to 2007, their conclusion that the broadening of electoral appeal is constrained to being within the ethnic community, rather than across ethnic communities),may be reasonable. However, I suggest here that the movement of ethnic parties toward becoming genuinely catch-all in the sense of appealing to out-group members may well be plausible, particularly for parties whose long-established reputations as moderates gives them greater credibility to reach across the divide. Hence, the parties in each bloc with conciliatory reputations—the UUP and SDLP—may reasonably be regarded as having at least some ethnic catch-all appeal. In the Catholic/ nationalist bloc, the SDLP has a strong reputation as a consistently constitutional party—very distinct from Sinn Féin, which has emerged from a violent nonconstitutional tradition. The SDLP has long fostered a policy of peaceful protest and engagement in dialogue with the representatives of the "rival" community (McLaughlin 2009). In the Protestant/unionist bloc, the UUP is typically regarded as the more conciliatory party. The party's perceived moderateness led to the establishment of the Democratic

Unionist Party in the early 1970s by Ian Paisley as a bulwark against any possible unionist compromise (see, for example, the discussion in Evans and Duffy 1997). Along with the SDLP, the UUP led the way in negotiating the 1998 Good Friday/Belfast Agreement, leading to the receipt of the Nobel Peace Prize by Hume and Trimble, respective party leaders.

Nationalist voters assessing the extent to which they support (or do not support) parties in the unionist bloc will, I suggest, be driven by their evaluations of the capabilities of the rival bloc parties to represent all groups in society. In assessing the ethnic catch-all abilities of the parties in the rival bloc, nationalist voters will be influenced by the party positions of the rival bloc parties. They may reason as follows: the UUP and the DUP currently hold moderate ethnonational positions. However, the UUP is a much more credible actor in terms of possibly representing fairly and competently the interests of all communities, because the UUP has a history of acting moderately, or at least more moderately than the DUP. Similarly, unionist voters assessing rival bloc parties are likely to regard Sinn Féin and the SDLP quite differently, given that the former party arose from a violent paramilitarism, in contrast to the consistent constitutionalism of the latter. Hence, the SDLP may be regarded as a much more credible performer of the ethnic catch-all function.

In essence, in the same way that Mitchell et al. (2009) argue that prior ethnonational position cues current (ethnic tribune) valence assessments and current within-bloc voting, I argue that prior ethnonational position cues current (ethnic catch-all) valence assessments and (potential cross-bloc) voting. The expectations to be empirically tested may be precisely stated. First, variation in Protestant citizens' likelihood of voting for the SDLP rather than Sinn Féin is a function of variation in Protestant citizens' relative evaluation of the capacity of the SDLP and Sinn Féin to perform the ethnic catch-all function. Second, variation in Catholic citizens' likelihood of voting for the UUP rather than the DUP is a function of variation in Catholic citizens' relative evaluation of the capacity of the UUP and the DUP to perform the ethnic catch-all function.

Measuring Potential Vote

Studies of voting behavior typically use vote choice as a dependent variable. Hence, voters are divided into a number of categories: assigned a 1 for the particular party they voted for and a 0 for all the other parties for which they did not vote. This categorical operationalization of voting behavior is almost ubiquitous and seemingly unproblematic. However, a number of analysts have emphasised the limited information yielded by such an operationalization of voting behavior (see discussion in van der Eijk 2002). The 1 versus 0 distinction does not capture the variation in the levels of support voters may have had for the range of parties in the system. One voter may well have no likelihood at all of voting for any of the parties for whom she did not vote. In contrast, another voter may have been torn between voting for parties A, B, and C; only very marginally preferring A, for whom she voted, to the other parties. The conventional operationalization of voting tells us nothing about the possibly nuanced set of views a voter may have about the range of parties in the system. In order to systematically measure voters' levels of support for all of the parties in the system a question wording has been developed, validated, and used in national and cross-national research projects. Applied to the Northern Ireland setting, the wording is as follows:

> There are a number of political parties in Northern Ireland, each of which would like to get your vote: How likely is it that you would ever vote for the following parties. Please indicate your views on this 1–10 scale, where 1 means not at all likely and 10 means very

likely. You may choose any number between 1 and 10. How likely is it that you would ever vote for [each party is listed and each party is separately scored by the respondent between 1 and 10].

The question is specifically designed not to act as a predictor variable (such as a party "likeability" or party sympathy scale). The wording directly relates to the act of voting rather than to any theoretical explanation of voting; hence it is designed as a nuanced measure of the variation in levels of electoral support that citizens have for the set of parties in their system (and is thus acting as a dependent rather than independent variable). Such measures, often referred to as "propensity to vote" measures, or more simply measures of "party support," have a range of advantages. Of particular import for present purposes is the detailed information such measures give us about parties not voted for. Crucially, in stark contrast to the conventional measure of vote choice, what these variables provide is information regarding citizens' levels of electoral support for parties in the rival bloc.

For present purposes it is the difference in likelihood of voting for the two rival-bloc parties that is important. Hence, for Protestant respondents, the likelihood of voting for Sinn Féin is subtracted from the likelihood of voting for the SDLP, resulting in a scale that theoretically runs from −9 to +9, higher scores representing a greater likelihood of voting for the SDLP than for Sinn Féin. For Catholic respondents, the likelihood of voting for the UUP is subtracted from the likelihood of voting for the DUP, resulting in a scale that theoretically runs from −9 to +9, higher scores representing a greater likelihood of voting for the UUP than for the DUP.

In order to measure ethnic catch-all evaluations, respondents were asked: How good is each party at representing the interests of both the Protestant community AND the Catholic community [1–10 scale, where 1 is "not good at all" and 10 is "very good']? It is the difference in the scores for rival bloc parties that it important for present purposes. Hence, similar to the above discussion regarding the construction of the dependent variables, Protestants' relative evaluations of the capacity of rival bloc parties to act as ethnic catch-all parties is generated by subtracting their score for Sinn Féin from their score for the SDLP, and Catholics' relative evaluations are generated by subtracting the DUP evaluation score from the UUP evaluation score.

Protestant Support for Rival Bloc Parties

Figures 5.2a and b show variation in Protestants' likelihood of voting for each of the nationalist parties. Very low levels of potential electoral support are evident from Protestants for Sinn Féin (73.5 percent indicated the lowest category (1)). In contrast, there is a much greater well of potential support for the SDLP (23 percent indicate a score of 6 or higher, and only 27 percent indicate the lowest possible score of 1). Figure 5.2c shows the variation in Protestants' relative support for the two nationalist parties, with positive scores indicating greater potential support for the SDLP than for Sinn Féin, negative scores indicating a preference for Sinn Féin over the SDLP, and a score of "0" indicating equal support levels for both parties. Clearly, there is quite a degree of variation in Protestants' relative propensity to vote for either Sinn Féin or the SDLP, and the balance of potential vote very clearly favors the SDLP.

The patterns in Figures 5.3a–c, which focus on ethnic catch-all capacity, are less stark but point in a similar direction. Thirty-six percent of Protestants indicate a score of six or higher for the SDLP, and only 5 percent give it the lowest possible score; in contrast, only 20 percent indicate a score of 6 or higher for Sinn Féin, and almost the same proportion give it the lowest score.

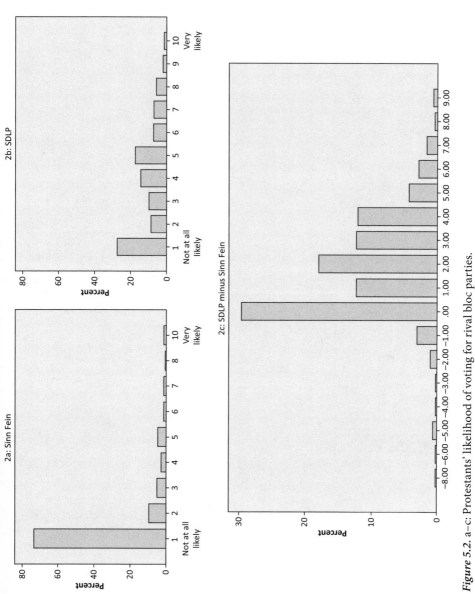

Figure 5.2. a–c: Protestants' likelihood of voting for rival bloc parties.

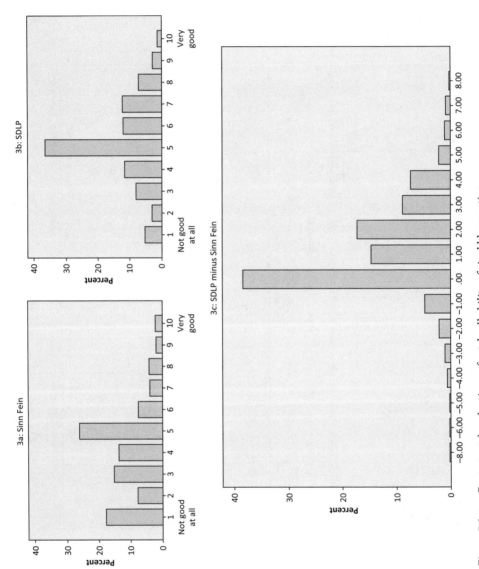

Figure 5.3. a–c Protestants' evaluations of catch-all ability of rival bloc parties.

Do relative catch-all evaluations predict relative party support, controlling for other relevant factors? The regression analysis reported in Appendix Table A5 suggests they do. The catch-all predictor is highly statistically significant and substantively very meaningful. This suggests that, controlling for other relevant factors, relative evaluations of rival-bloc parties' abilities to perform the ethnic catch-all function drive Protestants' relative likelihood of voting for the rival bloc parties.

Catholic Support for Rival Bloc Parties

Figures 5.4a and b show that the distribution of Catholic likelihood of voting for the DUP and UUP is very similar and largely negative. The amount of variation in Catholics' relative support for rival bloc parties (Figure 5.4c) is considerably less than the Protestant equivalent (Figure 5.2c above). More even distributions of opinion are evident in relation to the catch-all evaluations (Figures 5.5a, b). The relative catch-all evaluations of the two parties are illustrated in Figure 5.5c.

Does variation in Catholics' evaluations of the relative ethnic catch-all ability of rival- bloc parties predict Catholics' relative likelihood of voting for the UUP and DUP? The simple answer is no. The regression analysis—see Appendix Table A6—shows no statistically significant relationship.

Discussion

The asymmetric findings are interesting. Protestants clearly differentiate the two nationalist parties; they are considerably more likely to vote SDLP than Sinn Féin, and they are also considerably more likely to view SDLP, rather than Sinn Féin, as capable of representing both communities. Crucially, catch-all evaluations play a strong role in predicting relative propensity to vote for the two nationalist parties (while controlling for other

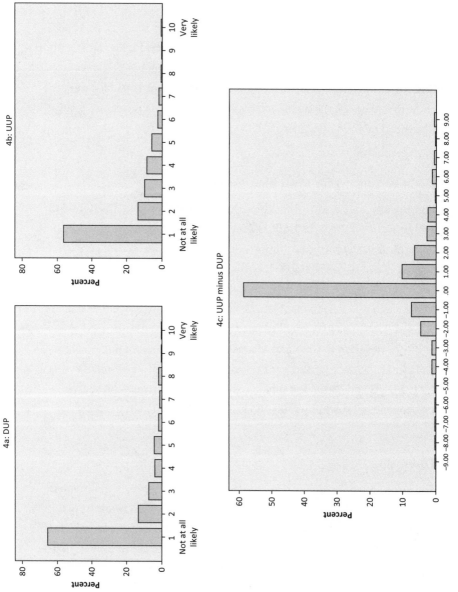

Figure 5.4. a–c: Catholics' likelihood of voting for rival bloc parties.

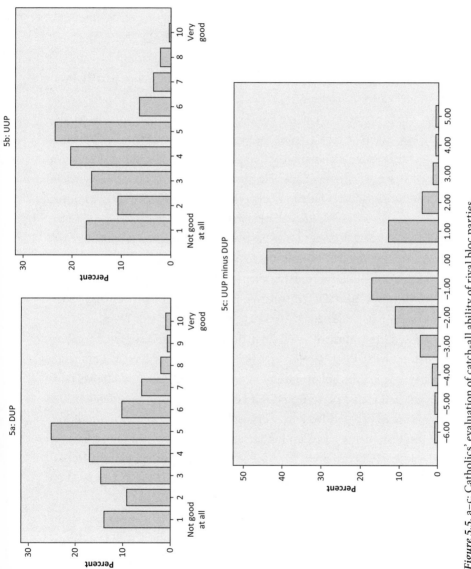

Figure 5.5. a–c: Catholics' evaluation of catch-all ability of rival bloc parties.

relevant explanatory factors). In contrast, Catholics clearly do not differentiate much between the DUP and UUP in terms of likelihood of voting for either party, and actually slightly favor the DUP over the UUP in terms of the catch-all role. Crucially, catch-all evaluations play no role in explaining relative propensity to vote for the two unionist parties. Protestants' views of nationalist parties are thus very different from Catholics' views of unionist parties. For Protestants the two nationalist parties are very different; for Catholics the two unionist parties are very similar.

One possible explanation of the asymmetric results is that the historical differences between Sinn Féin and the SDLP have been much greater than the historical differences between the UUP and DUP, hence leading to Protestants clearly differentiating the two nationalist parties and Catholics not clearly differentiating the two unionist parties. As noted in earlier chapters, in terms of attitudes to political violence and determination to achieve long-term constitutional goals, several analysts have noted that the Sinn Féin/SDLP distinction is more potent than the DUP/ UUP distinction (Coakley 2008; McGarry and O'Leary 2009). The paramilitarism and irredentism of Sinn Féin in the pre-peace process period arguably enabled the SDLP to develop a particularly clear reputation as a moderate party; the SDLP's abhorrence of violence rendered it a qualitatively different nationalist party from Sinn Féin. In contrast, the differences between the UUP and DUP were arguably a matter of degree of unionism, rather than being based on fundamentally different positions regarding the acceptability of political violence that distinguished nationalist parties. Somewhat speculatively, this suggests a resketching of Figure 5.1 (as presented in Figure 5.6).

The asymmetric finding may also be consistent with analyses of vote transfers in Northern Ireland's elections held under the Single Transferable Vote system. Elliot (2009), for example, finds evidence of cross-community transfers from the main unionist parties and from the main

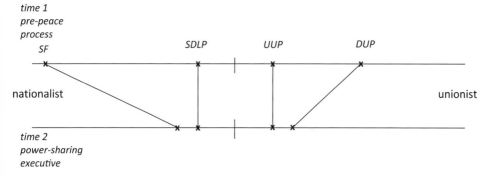

Figure 5.6. Asymmetric sketch of party position.

nationalist parties. However, the former tend to be stronger than the latter, and the transfers to the SDLP from the UUP were the most sizeable. Elliot analysed transfers in 1998, 2003, and 2007 Assembly elections and, in each case, reports higher unionist to nationalist transfers than the reverse, and particularly UUP to SDLP transfers in all three elections (noteworthy, also, is the DUP to SDLP transfers that were nontrivial in 2007) (Elliot 2009: Tables 1–3).

The more general implication of the asymmetric findings is that they act as a caution against assuming symmetry in party competition in deeply divided places. In each competing bloc in a deeply divided system, there will be a party with the staunchest views, and these parties are often described similarly as the "extreme" parties in the system in contrast to the "moderate" parties (those parties in each bloc with less staunch views). However, the two so-called "extreme" parties may be looked upon very differently by citizens in the opposing community. The evidence in this chapter suggests that one community may clearly differentiate rival bloc parties in terms of how likely they would be to support the different parties, and this variation in support is driven by judgments about the relative capacity of the parties to represent all groups. In contrast, another community may see very little difference between the so-called "moderate" and "extreme" parties in the opposing bloc, and this may perhaps be accounted for by the fact that the differences between opposing bloc parties were never so great (for example, there was not a distinction between a violent and nonviolent party).Hence, differences between the parties in terms of their relative credibility regarding the catch-all function were never likely to be large or electorally potent.

A final point relates to methodological implications. Most analysts of electoral behavior use categorical vote choice as the dependent variable. Here, it is potential voting that was focused on. The survey questions asked how likely it is a respondent would ever vote for each of the parties in the system, on a 10-point scale. This nuanced question has been used as the dependent variable in voting studies by a growing number of researchers (for overview see van der Eijk and Franklin 2009). It is a particularly useful question in a deeply divided place, because it captures the difference between some voters who would never vote for a particular "rival" ethnic party and other voters who possibly would. Identifying the extent of potential cross-bloc party support and understanding the motivations of potential cross-divide voters is a prerequisite for understanding the possibilities for electoral change in deeply divided contexts. It is extremely difficult to conduct such an investigation with the category-based conventionally operationalized dependent variable in voting studies, given that such a variable does not directly capture variation in the propensity to vote for parties. Hence, the more widespread use of the nuanced measures used in this study is advocated in order to aid understanding of electoral politics deeply divided places.

Understanding Nonparticipation

The previous four chapters have focused on the voting behavior of Northern Ireland citizens and have tried to understand the determinants of party support. In this chapter the focus of attention is on whether or not citizens actually participate at election time. This is a particularly pressing issue, as nonvoting in Northern Ireland is of increasing concern to policy makers, with participation levels falling from an initial high of 70 percent in the first Assembly election of 1998 to a low of 57 percent in 2011 (see Figure 6.1).

The fact that turnout significantly declined may have come as no surprise to some critics of consociation who characterize power-sharing arrangements as elitist and exclusionary. They argue that consociation's focus on negotiations between party leaders, rather than on ordinary citizens and civil society group members, leads to citizens feeling distanced from the creation and maintenance of the new institutional order. Such alienation may lead to strong emotional antipathy to the parties in the system that allegedly seek to represent the citizens. Furthermore, the keenness of consociationalists to incorporate as many parties as possible in a power-sharing coalition leads, it is argued, to government by cozy cartel. There is little room for opposition, and little chance of replacing the government with a different one, so why should citizens bother to engage at election time, as their vote will make little difference to the outcome,

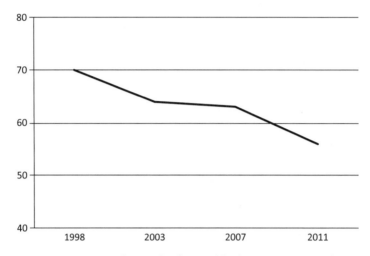

Figure 6.1. Turnout at Northern Ireland Assembly elections, 1998–2011 (percent).

which inevitably will be extremely similar to the outcome of the previous election?

A pro-consociational response to these concerns may be that 57 percent is still a fairly healthy turnout rate by international standards. Also, consociational power sharing should be seen as inclusionary rather than exclusionary, in that party supporters see their favored party's votes translated directly into parliamentary seats and executive portfolios. More generally, consociationalists may point out that alienation levels are commonplace across modern democracies and cannot be blamed on consociational arrangements.

This chapter seeks to shed empirical light on the drivers of nonparticipation in Northern Ireland and in so doing to identify the elements, if any, of the critics' arguments that are supported. The chapter begins with a general typology of the drivers of participation, in the context of which the specific Northern Irish consociational context is situated. Two interpretations of nonvoting in Northern Ireland are then elaborated and tested: an emotional/psychological interpretation (citizens feel alienated by the focus on party elites and hence abstain) and a rational interpretation focusing on the difficulties of responsibility attribution (the all-inclusive power-sharing system is too complicated and therefore citizens abstain).

A Typology of Participation

In order to understand why some citizens participate at election time and others do not, it is useful to start by distinguishing between two distinct types of non-voters. First, "circumstantial abstention" relates to voters who would have liked to vote but circumstances on the day of the election prevented them from doing so. Such circumstances may relate to being away from home, or having pressing work or family commitments, or being ill on the day of the election. In contrast, "voluntary abstention" relates to the attitudes that citizens have which lead them not to vote. For example, low levels of political efficacy—a lack of interest in politics, or a sense that one will have little influence on the outcome of the election—are likely to be related to abstention, as is an individual's lack of an emotional attachment to any political party (see discussion in Marsh et al. 2008).

The problem of circumstantial abstention may be addressed by generating a context which makes the act of voting as easy as possible. For instance, having voting on a Sunday, or over two days, may help individuals whose work or family commitments might otherwise prevent them from voting. The problem of voluntary abstention may be addressed by generating a context in which citizens are mobilized and persuaded to turn out to vote. For instance, a very close election in which intense campaigning

Type of influence	Location of the factor	
	Contextual level	Individual level
Facilitation *(making it easy to vote)*	*contextual facilitation*	*Individual facilitation*
	contextual factors that make it easy for people to vote	factors relating to an individual's circumstances that make it easy to vote
	(e.g., voting on a Sunday or over the whole weekend)	(e.g., not being ill on election, day, having flexible working)
Mobilization *(making people want to vote)*	*contextual mobilization*	*individual mobilization*
	contextual factors making people want to vote	characteristics of individuals that make them want to vote
	(e.g., clarity of responsibility across coalition parties and across levels of government)	(e.g., positive psychological identification with a party or parties)

Figure 6.2. Typology of factors driving participation (derived from Marsh et al. 2008).

increases people's interest may raise turnout. Also, a context in which there are very clear differences between parties may make it seem worthwhile to vote. Figure 6.2 seeks to link the contextual and individual level drivers of turnout by offering a typology of the factors which affect participation, distinguishing the role of mobilization and facilitation.

The focus here is on the bottom two quadrants of the typology: the challenge of ensuring, at the individual level, that voters feel that they want to vote, and the challenge, at the contextual level, of ensuring that the political context encourages them to want to vote.

Emotions and Participation

In their seminal analysis of voting behavior in the United States, Campbell et al. (1960) sought to explain the long-term stability of party support using the concept of "party identification," which refers to citizens' general and enduring psychological orientations toward the political parties in the system. The authors defined the concept as follows (1960: 121–22):

> In characterizing the relation of individual to party as a psychological identification we invoke a concept that has played an important if somewhat varied role in psychological theories of the relation of individual to individual or of individual to group. We use the concept here to characterize the individual's affective orientation to an important group-object in his environment. Both reference group theory and small-group studies of influence have converged upon the attracting or repelling quality of the group as the generalized dimension most critical in defining the individual-group relationship, and it is this dimension that we will call identification . . . the political party serves as the group towards which the individual may develop an identification, positive or negative, of some degree of intensity.

Thus, party identification relates to a psychological rather than behavioral relationship between a citizen and the parties; it is subjective and based on self-definition rather than a result of voting for the party. Crucially, for present purposes, this definition suggests that party identification may be negative or positive, with certain parties perceived as either attractive or repellent, and citizens may identify with more than one party. However, this contrasts with the usual way party identification is operationalized, which facilitates only a positive attachment to a particular party and prohibits multiple attachments. Accordingly, Campbell et al. (1960: 121–22) use the following measure:

> Generally speaking, do you usually think of yourself as a Republican, a Democrat, an Independent, or what? Respondents identifying with one of the two parties are then asked: "Would you call yourself a strong Democrat (or Republican) or a not very strong Democrat (or Republican)?" Respondents who identify as Independents in the initial question are asked: Do you think of yourself as closer to the Republican or Democratic Party?

This measure is criticized by Maggiotto and Pierson (1977), who argue in favor of "the addition of partisan hostility, an equally stable, long term affect" (765). Similarly, Richardson (1991: 759) highlights the theoretical and explanatory value of negative as well as positive identity: "hostility to parties other than favored ones may be as important behaviorally as positive ties to liked parties." In a recent analysis, Medeiros and Noël (2014) emphasize the important "autonomous" role played by negative partisanship, which they characterize as "the forgotten side of partisanship" in driving electoral behavior.

Furthermore, several analysts have emphasized that many citizens may have multiple identifications. Weisberg (1999: 727) notes that analyses of party identification in the U.S.-based on this Campbell et al. (1960) measure "have assumed that people are Republicans or Democrats or Independents, but not more than one of the above," and such analyses represent a quite limited operationalization of their general concept of party identification, as it does not facilitate the holding of multiple identities by individuals. In a similar vein, van der Eijk and Niemöller (1983) argue that "the assumption that voters identify with only one party (if they do so at all) turns out to be false when subjected to an empirical test in the

Netherlands" (338). Also, Schmitt (2002) states that "multiple party identifications are indeed a relevant aspect of partisanship. Noteworthy proportions of national electorates identify with more than one political
party" (19).

Conceptualizing party identification in terms of positive and negative identification and in terms of multiple identification is likely to be
particularly useful in the context of analyzing participation in a consociational polity. Such a context is typically characterized as comprising a
number of party systems—one for each of the rival communities—and
party competition occurs within each community bloc. Multiple party
identities may well be plausible in such a setting. In the same way as Weisberg (1999: 727) notes that Dutch citizens who identify with one of the
Dutch Calvinist parties may also identify with the other Dutch Calvinist
party, one might expect that some Catholics may positively identify with
both the "Catholic" parties.

It may also be the case that at least some Catholics would negatively
identify with both the Catholic parties. The same may well be true for
Protestants—at least some Protestants may negatively identify with both
main "Protestant parties." The aim here is to empirically assess the relationship between multiple negative identification and abstention. Is
emotional alienation from the community bloc parties responsible for
low turnout levels? (See Garry 2015 for an elaborated version of the argument in this section; also Garry 2007.)

I construct a measure of affective party identification for the deeply
divided Northern Ireland context that facilitates multiple identification
and positive and negative identification. The battery of survey items is
"Some people feel close to a particular political party while other people
feel distant from it. Taking each party in turn, do you feel very close to
the party, fairly close, neither close nor distant, fairly distant from the
party or very distant from it? [all parties asked in turn]." The responses to

Table 6.1. Catholics' Psychological Attachment to Sinn Féin and SDLP (%)

| | | Sinn Féin | | |
		close to	neither	distant from
	close to	16.3	10.8	13.5
SDLP	neither	7.5	26.5	2.1
	distant from	6.3	1.0	16.1

Total $n = 480$.

each party identification question are recoded into three categories: positive identification (very close or fairly close to), neutral identification (neither close to nor distant from) and negative identification (fairly or very distant from). Each community (Catholics and Protestants) was then analyzed in turn. First, the manner in which citizens identify with the two parties in their community was assessed. Then, the percentage turnout for each party identification category was investigated in order to assess the extent to which multiple negative identification drives abstention. In Table 6.1 we see that 16 percent of Catholics hold multiple positive identifications: they feel close to both their community parties (Sinn Féin and the SDLP). The same percentage hold multiple negative identifications: regarding both parties as repellent. The largest category, slightly over a quarter of Catholics, are neutral toward both parties.

In Table 6.2 the percentage of citizens in each cell who participated in the 2011 Assembly election is reported. Citizens who are close to at least one party (and who may be close to, distant from, or neutral regarding the other party) have turnout rates of at least 70 percent. A slightly lower rate (63 percent) is indicated in relation to those who are neutral regarding both parties. However, the stark finding in the table relates to the very low (37.7 percent) turnout rate of those citizens who negatively identify with both parties.

Table 6.2. Catholic Turnout by Catholics' Psychological Attachment to Sinn Féin and SDLP (%)

| | | Sinn Féin | | |
		close to	*neither*	*distant from*
	close to	74.4	75.0	70.1
SDLP	neither	75.0	63.0	**
	distant from	83.3	**	37.7

Figure in each cell is percentage turnout; ** indicates too few cases, in all other cells minimum *n* = 30.

Table 6.3. Protestants' Psychological Attachment to UUP and DUP (%)

| | | UUP | | |
		close to	*neither*	*distant from*
	close to	21.6	7.8	8.1
DUP	neither	4.2	27.0	1.5
	distant from	6.6	1.9	21.3

Total *n* = 670.

Table 6.3 reports the distribution of Protestant voters regarding their psychological relationship with the two main parties in the "unionist" bloc. The distribution is somewhat similar to the Catholic case (Table 6.1). Just over a fifth of Protestants have multiple positive identifications with the parties, just over a fifth have multiple negative identifications, and just over a quarter have a neutral identification with the parties.

Table 6.4 reports the turnout percentage in each cell. The pattern that emerges is similar to, but less stark than, the Catholic case. The highest turnout percentages (57–71 percent) are for those Protestants who positively identify with at least one party. The lowest turnout is for those with multiple negative identifications (45.5 percent), but the percentage is

Table 6.4. Protestant Turnout by Protestant Psychological Attachment to UUP and DUP (%)

		UUP		
		close to	*neither*	*distant from*
	close to	66.9	57.7	61.6
DUP	neither	71.4	47.0	**
	distant from	56.8	**	45.5

Figure in each cell is percentage turnout; ** indicates too few cases, in all other cells minimum $n = 28$.

very similar to that for those who have neutral identities with both (47.0 percent).

Thus, the overall picture is that psychological attachment to the parties in one's community bloc influences the decision to participate. For Catholics, antipathy to both bloc parties strongly drives abstention: multiple antipathy turnout rates are only half of multiple closeness turnout rates. The same trend, though less strong, is evident for Protestants. A key difference between Catholics and Protestants, which helps account for higher overall participation rates of Catholics, is that Catholics who are psychologically neutrally disposed toward both their bloc parties are much more likely to participate than Protestants who are neutral toward both their parties; indifference to parties is related to nonparticipation for Protestants but not for Catholics.

Attribution Difficulties and Participation

Another model is also tested that assumes it is simply too difficult for citizens to attribute responsibility. The model assumes that voters become so confused and frustrated by the challenge of attributing responsibility that they simply do not bother to vote at all. This model sees the vertical distribution of power and the horizontal sharing of power as contributing to citizen apathy and abstention by making political life so much more complicated than the "simple" operation of a two-party system in a unitary state.

Cutler (2008: 630) comments that, in response to confusion regarding responsibility in the multilevel government context, voters "might throw up their hands, saying "why bother voting in this election when I can't tell whether this government is responsible for any of the things I care about?" This speculation is consistent with the aggregate-level findings of Henderson and McEwan (2010), who analyzed variation in turnout across regional elections and found a relationship between high levels of regional autonomy and high levels of regional turnout, suggesting that when regional government is seen by citizens to have significant power citizens are inclined to turn out to vote. These aggregate-level findings still leave open the question of individual-level variation in turnout, which is likely to be linked to variation between individuals in terms of the extent to which they regard their regional government as powerful: those citizens who attribute a lot of political responsibility to the regional government are arguably more likely to turn out to vote than those citizens who do not see the regional government as possessing much power, and hence do not attribute to it much responsibility.

The addition of further ambiguity relating to the horizontal level (sharing of power between coalition parties) may incentivize abstention even farther. For example, Brokington (2004: 473) suggests that deciding how to vote in a coalition context represents a "complex task environment" in which "responsibility for policy failure is difficult to ascribe to a single party." This leads to "a deterioration in external efficacy or the sense that the government is responsive to the desires of the electorate. This reduces the potential benefits of casting a ballot, and therefore the probability of participation" (473). In a similar vein, Karp and Banducci (2008:

332) find empirical support "for the assumption that broad coalition governments depress efficacy which can discourage voter participation." The expectation then is that citizens who attribute responsibility vertically and horizontally are less likely to abstain than citizens who do not attribute responsibility.

In order to assess whether perceptions of the vertical distribution of power drive turnout, a scale was generated in which a high score represented a tendency by respondents to attribute responsibility to the Northern Ireland government for each of the seven issue areas discussed in Chapter 4, and a low score represented a tendency to indicate that the Northern Ireland government was not responsible. The scale runs from zero (Northern Ireland government not perceived to be responsible for any of the issue areas) to seven (Northern Ireland government perceived to be responsible for all seven issue areas). As reported in model 1 in Appendix Table A7, this variable does not predict the decision not to vote in 2011.

A scale was also generated which measured respondents' ability to attribute power horizontally. As noted, respondents who indicated that the Northern Ireland government was responsible for a particular issue area were then asked to indicate which party, or parties, were most responsible. Respondents who did not indicate a particular party either responded "don't know" or "all parties are equally responsible." Respondents who indicated, for each issue area, that "all parties are equally responsible" were coded "1," other respondents were coded "0." The resulting seven dichotomous variables were summed to generate a 0–7 scale, higher scores indicating a tendency to regard all parties as equally responsible. Again, this variable does not predict the decision not to vote (model 2 in Appendix 6.1).

Also, a dichotomous variable was created from the two questions asking about the influence of the two unionist parties: citizens who perceived both parties to be of equal influence versus citizens who perceived one of the parties to be more influential than the other. A similar measure was created for the parties in the nationalist bloc. These variables were used to predict abstention, but none emerged as statistically significant predictors (as reported in models 3 and 4 in Appendix 6.1).

Discussion

In trying to understand abstention in Northern Ireland, this chapter takes as its departure point the general argument of critics that consociational settlements are elitist in character and serve to alienate ordinary citizens. This general concern is then allied to particular aspects of the Northern Ireland consociational institutions in order to generate specific expectations regarding the drivers of abstention. First, the Northern Ireland version of consociation is regional and complete, leading to—respectively—the challenge of attributing political responsibility across levels of government and across the full range of parties in the power-sharing government. The ultra-inclusiveness of the power-sharing executive, allied to its devolved nature, may result in many citizens being overwhelmed by the complexity. Not being able to clearly discern where power lies, such citizens decide to stay at home at election time. Empirically, no evidence was found to support this interpretation. Voters were just as likely as non-voters to see the system as highly complex; perceiving complexity did not deter them from participating.

A second investigation focused on the notion of party blocs, the idea that there is one set of parties for Catholics and one set of parties for Protestants. This characterization of party competition as divided into two party systems (one for each community group) is, according to critics of consociation, accentuated by the designation mechanism which incentivizes community members to vote within their respective blocs. But what about citizens who are emotionally antipathetic toward both the main parties in "their" bloc? Such emotional reaction may lead to a disengagement from the political system altogether. Empirical evidence was found to support the link between multiple negative identity with bloc parties and abstention. In particular, Catholic multiple negative identifiers were unlikely to vote.

Chapter 7

Conclusions

The three main criticisms of the consociational response to conflict have, as elaborated in Chapter 1, implications for the nature of party competition and electoral behavior. Are those implications observable in the Northern Ireland case? Chapters 2 and 3 assessed the role of ethnonational ideology, suggested by critics to suffocate all other potential policy dimensions. Chapters 4 and 5 examined the possibility of electoral accountability, suggested by critics to be impossible. Chapter 6 examined electoral participation, suggested by critics to be low due to citizen disengagement resulting from the elites-focus of consociation or the complexity of power sharing. In the first part of this Conclusion I summarize the main empirical findings. In the second part I elaborate the implications of the findings for assessments of the quality of electoral democracy associated with consociational design. Finally, I suggest a number of avenues for further research that could add to our understanding of electoral democracy under consociational conditions.

Main Findings

Dominance of Ethnonational Ideology?

Chapter 2 demonstrated that voting is very strongly driven by ethnonational factors. First, in relation to party-bloc voting, very few Catholics vote for either of the two unionist parties, and very few Protestants vote for either of the two nationalist parties. This continues the long-observed trend of "religious" voting in Northern Ireland. It is thus clear that in terms of first-preference vote choice a fully functioning consociational system has not prompted significant sections of either community to vote "across the divide." There is considerable heterogeneity, however, within each community bloc. The often assumed mapping of Catholic/ Irish/nationalist/pro-united Ireland versus Protestant/British/unionist/ pro-integration into the UK does not emerge. Instead, a lot more fluidity is evident, and in relation to identity, ideological self-description, and long-term constitutional preferences a trichotomy rather than dichotomy on each point is necessary. In addition to British and Irish identity, a "Northern Irish" identity is important, attracting a significant minority of each community. Also, more than two-fifths of each community describe themselves as "neither unionist nor nationalist." Regarding long-term preferences, a minority of Catholics seek a united Ireland and a minority of Protestants seek integration into the UK; the status quo— devolved power sharing—is the majority preference of both communities. Hence, in each community the distinction to be made is not so much between citizens with very strong versus moderate ethnonationalism but between those who have an ethnonational position and those who do not. Hence, many Catholics are not "Irish," not in favor of a united Ireland, and not nationalist. They tend to vote SDLP. The distinction is not so electorally potent on the Protestant side.

The stark dichotomous distinctions often made about ethnonationalism in Northern Ireland should be replaced with three-way distinctions to capture the large proportion of each community who do not hold the "predictable" ethnonational positions and instead hold a neutral position. This fluidity is not consistent with the "freezing" criticism, suggesting

that consociational arrangements do not act as a constraint on the melting of ethnonational distinctions.

Critics are correct, however, in that there is little evidence of other
political dimensions such as economic left-right (or moral conservative-
liberal) emerging. The one important and intriguing exception here relates
to the pro- versus anti-EU dimension. Northern Ireland may be characterized as a consociation within a consociation, given that the EU has
been interpreted as a consociational polity (Bogaards and Crepaz 2002).
In elections to the European Parliament, parties in one community bloc
do offer a clear choice, with the relatively skeptical Sinn Féin vying with
enthusiast SDLP. Pro-EU Catholics vote for the latter at the EP election,
and skeptics for the former. However, the pro- versus anti-EU distinction
does not drive Catholic choice at the non-EP elections. This suggests that
a cross-cutting dimension of political competition can be potent, when
parties offer a choice and the issue is made at least somewhat salient. Being the bottom rung of a multilevel consociation may thus help lessen the
salience of ethnonational competition by providing an externally generated cross-cutting divide.

The absence of an economic left-right or class-based dimension of
competition will be of particular concern to some critics, who regard such
a dimension of competition as more "normal" or "progressive" than
identity-based competition. Some have argued that the simplest way to
replace ethnonational competition with class-based competition is full
electoral integration into the UK. If the "class-based" competition between Labour and the Conservatives could be brought to all parts of the
UK, then identity-based competition in Northern Ireland would melt
away as elections become dominated by class-related issues. Prior to the
IRA ceasefires Duffy and Evans's (1997) analysis suggests this was not a
very likely scenario and not a good alternative to the "peace process." In

a very different political world I updated and extended the Duffy and Evans analysis. The relevant question now is not whether electoral integration would provide an alternative to power sharing, but whether electoral integration could aid a transition toward a politics based, as critics would like, on class and economic ideological differences. I found remarkably similar results for the Conservatives and Labour, as Duffy and Evans did. Catholics are much more likely to support Labour than the Conservatives, and the reverse is true for Protestants. However, there are two ways to think about bringing British party competition to Northern Ireland; in terms of the set of parties (Labour versus Conservatives), or simply in terms of a single party. While Labour and the Conservatives, as just noted, attract different community support, the Labour party is much more able than the Conservatives to attract cross-community support. Thus, from the perspective of an electoral integrationist who wishes to see a diminution of community voting via the use of British parties, bringing in the Labour party and not the Conservatives is clearly the best option. The reverse, of course, is what is actually happening: the Conservatives are organizing and competing in Northern Ireland, and Labour refuses to do so, much to the annoyance of Northern Ireland Labour members. Two important caveats should be entered about the potential role of Labour. The party's involvement would come at the cost of cross-community or moderate parties. Alliance and the SDLP would suffer significantly. Furthermore, there is little evidence that there is a class/ economic ideology basis to Labour support in Northern Ireland. Hence, its involvement may be to the cost of existing moderate Northern Ireland parties without bringing the "benefit" of class-based politics to Northern Ireland.

A better bet would seem to be the Liberal Democrats. They take support from the biconfessional Alliance, but they do bring a class politics. It is, however, somewhat different from the classic working-class/leftist versus middle-class/rightist distinction. Liberal Democrat supporters tend to be middle-class leftists, and might well simply approximate Alliance, its "sister" party, by another name.

Electoral integration with the Republic of Ireland is also interesting to consider. Protestants, unsurprisingly, do not like Irish parties, while Catholics are somewhat supportive. Fianna Fáil (the Republican party) is the most ethnonationally rooted in a Northern Ireland support base. There is an economic policy basis to Fianna Fáil and Labour support. If the aim of electoral integrationists is to import economic policy-based party competition into Northern Ireland, then integrating with the Republic of Ireland may serve the purpose just as well as integrating with the rest of Britain.

These counterfactuals are interesting for contemporary Northern Ireland politics. If the consociational power-sharing settlement has achieved the primary aim of achieving security and political stability, then there is calm space for considering how politics can "progress," and the potential role of British and Irish parties is one of these ways.

No Electoral Accountability?

Critics suggest that consociational arrangements cannot credibly be regarded as democratic, as there is no clear distinction between government and opposition, and no way for citizens to throw out a poorly performing government and replace it with a different one. Governments cannot change in a consociation; the same parties simply stay in power, and elections make little or no difference. This interpretation is quite damning, as it implies that consociation is a quasi-authoritarian regime with an enduring elite that is beyond the reach of ordinary citizens who wish to hold it to account for its behavior. The consociational response to this criticism is simple: in Northern Ireland there are elections, the

PR-STV electoral system used is widely regarded as the one giving the greatest possible range of choice to voters, there is fierce intra-community party competition, and voters are free to choose between parties on the basis of citizens' evaluations of each party's performance in government. This process is unlikely to lead to the replacement of one government with a different one, but it facilitates significant change in the relative size of parties in office. Hence, electoral accountability is challenging but far from impossible.

The difficulties relating to voters holding governments to account have attracted a lot of analysis. Ease of accountability varies considerably across institutional context. The greater the horizontal and vertical sharing of power, the greater the challenge for voters to discern which particular political actors are responsible. The complete and regional nature of the Northern Ireland consociational arrangements accentuates this difficulty, making Northern Ireland an extremely challenging case in which to observe electoral accountability in operation. It is therefore meaningful that at least some electoral accountability was observed.

The difficulties relate to the wide range of parties on offer: how to discern who is responsible for what? To offset this there are factors that should signal to voters the relative influence of parties in the executive: relative size as measured by number of portfolios, and whether or not a party holds one of the co-premier positions. Accordingly, Sinn Féin and the DUP were much more influential than the UUP or SDLP, an interpretation strongly perceived by citizens to be accurate. Also, the parties, via the d'Hondt portfolio distribution mechanism, hold distinct cabinet posts, and some of these signal to voters that that party is especially responsible for that particular policy area.

Overall, and issue-specific, electoral accountability is evident in the Protestant-bloc choice between UUP and DUP. The DUP is rewarded by those Protestants who positively evaluated the overall government performance and perceived the DUP to be particularly influential in government. Also, relatively positive evaluation of how Protestants' interests have been protected during the governing period leads to support for the DUP, but only for those Protestants who perceive the DUP to be particularly responsible for representing Protestant interests.

This concern regarding the representation of community interests is also investigated with regard to citizens' views of parties in the "rival" bloc. Do citizens perceive that rival-bloc parties can perform the function of looking after the interests of all groups in Northern Ireland? How likely are citizens to vote across the divide? Is likelihood of voting across the divide driven by perceptions of how well rival parties would perform in terms of representing all communities? The evidence of Chapter 4 suggests that the role of the SDLP is particularly interesting. There is evidence of significant potential Protestant support for the SDLP, support driven by a positive evaluation of the SDLP's ability to represent both Protestants and Catholics. Protestants' views of Sinn Féin and Catholic views of both the UUP and the DUP are negative in terms of likelihood of supporting the parties and belief that the parties could perform the ethnic catch-all function.

Asymmetry

The findings just described are strongly asymmetric. There is much more evidence of issue voting in the Catholic bloc than in the Protestant bloc, and much more evidence of performance voting in the Protestant bloc than the Catholic bloc. The nature of the difference between the parties in each bloc may explain this. The difference between Sinn Féin and the SDLP was qualitative rather than being a matter of degree. Sinn Féin's violent nationalism was distinct from the constitutional nationalism of the SDLP. This major distinction contrasts with the differences in the unionist bloc, which mainly centered on the acceptability of a power-sharing settlement. Once the DUP accepted power sharing with Sinn Féin, the UUP-DUP differences were minimal on constitutional matters. In contrast, the long-term constitutional question differentiates the SDLP and Sinn Féin, the latter being more stridently pro-united Ireland than the former. This drives within-community vote choice, and also drives Protestant potential cross-bloc vote choice. The UUP-DUP similarity means that ethnonational position does not drive within- community vote choice, nor does it differentiate regarding Catholic views of unionist parties.

It is valence-based politics which is electorally potent in the unionist bloc. While similar on ethnonational position, the DUP is seen to be more closely associated with representing Protestant interests in the power-sharing executive than is the UUP. This arguably suggests that there is more political space for valence-related performance-based politics in the particular community in which the parties' ethnonational positions are similar, while performance politics is more constrained in the community in which the parties still hold distinct ethnonational positions, due to past behavior or future preferences.

Elite Driven and Undermines Participation?

A final criticism of consociation relates to its allegedly elitist nature and its exclusion of ordinary citizens. Consociationalists prioritize a power-sharing settlement negotiated between the leaders of rival communities and do not emphasize the need for a grassroots-based approach to conflict resolution. Focusing on elites may alienate ordinary citizens, leaving them feeling distant from the parties in their bloc that seek to represent them. A consequence may be disaffection with the system as a whole and a disinclination to participate at election time. There was some evidence suggesting this, particularly in the Catholic bloc. Although the proportion of Catholics with a negative emotional relationship with both the SDLP and Sinn Féin was quite low (16 percent), the Catholics in this group were particularly unlikely to vote at election time. There was a somewhat higher percentage of Protestants with multiple negative identification with both unionist parties (DUP and UUP), but this distance from both parties did not lead this group of Protestants to be especially likely to abstain. Overall, there is some Catholic disaffection with "Catholic parties" which leads to abstention.

Is the decline in turnout due to citizens feeling overwhelmed by the complexity of the system and deciding to no longer vote? The analysis suggests not. Although regional and complete consociation are undoubtedly challenging for voters in terms of discerning in whose hands exactly power lies, this challenge does not seem to result in the decision to give up on the system and abstain.

Implications for the Study of Other Consociational Polities

While this study is a large-N study in terms of representative sampling and the number of respondents, it is—in another crucial respect"—an N of 1. The focus is on one particular case of consociational democracy, at one particular period of time (a snapshot, albeit one with a parliamentary term length of exposure). The extent to which one can generalize from one particular case is obviously limited. What is valuable about a single case study, however, is the ability to conduct in-depth analysis of the particular mechanisms at play in a particular type of consociational democracy. These mechanisms may be of use in terms of illuminating political processes of attitude formation and political behavior that are relevant in consociational democracies more broadly. The book has illustrated four particular mechanisms of interest.

Issues-Valence Link and "Ethnic Catch-All" Parties

The distinction between issue voting and valence voting is now commonplace in studies of electoral behavior and dates back to Donald Stokes's critique of Anthony Downs's policy- position-based rational choice approach to party competition and voting. The distinction, from the voters' perspective, is between asking the following two questions: 1) which party agrees with me? and 2) which party is most efficient? This distinction is helpful in the context of the emergence of a fully functioning consociational system because, as Mitchell et al. (2009) have argued, once all parties agree to share power what becomes important is not issues relating to the constitution, but rather group representation in the executive. Hence, the citizen no longer calculates "which party agrees with me on the constitutional question" but rather calculates "now that power sharing is operating, which party will most efficiently represent my community in the government?" Parties previously seen as hardline on the constitutional question will have an advantage in terms of now being seen as the most efficient at representing group interests. I extend this Mitchell et al. argument by focusing not on group interests but on the interests of all groups, and suggest that prior constitutional position does produce a valence advantage for long- time moderate parties such as SDLP and UUP. Only in relation to the SDLP did this actually emerge empirically. But the mechanism at play—prior position conditioning current ethnic catch-all valence advantage—is relevant to consider for any power-sharing polity.

Potential Vote and Non-Bloc Parties

Measuring party support using a scale that captures how likely it is that you would ever vote for a particular party is extremely useful when engaging in counterfactual analysis. In this book potential vote was used in two ways: first, to investigate the ethnonational and class basis of support for British and Irish parties, and second, to investigate the role of ethnic-catch all evaluations in driving support for rival bloc parties. Incorporating these two notions of voting (actual vote choice and potential party support) into studies of divided places, including consociational polities, can extend the analyst's toolkit, allowing the analyst to get a sense of the extent to which the current system of electoral support is rigid or possibly open to change. This is particularly important in consociational democracy, as openness to change is one of the key sources of interest.

Attribution of Responsibility When Power Is Shared

The notion of electoral accountability is often discussed in overly simple terms. The precise mechanisms at play in holding a government to account at election time are twofold. First, citizens must identify what it is that the government is actually responsible for. This isn't straightforward in a highly interdependent globalized world, especially in the multilevel-government context. Second, having identified what it is that the government has power over, the particular elements of the government wielding the power must be identified. After all, people do not vote for governments at election time, they vote for parties. Aside from the rare cases of single-party government, citizens must try and identify which constituent part of the government (i.e., which party) is most responsible, or is responsible for particular issue domains of interest. Any sensible model of electoral democracy takes these two allocations of responsibility into account before linking citizens' evaluations of performance to their vote choice. Regional and complete consociation, as in the Northern Ireland case, represents an extreme case of the difficulties associated with attributing responsibility across two power-sharing levels: vertical (multilevel government) and horizontal (coalition government). Discussions of the operation of electoral accountability in other consociational democracies may usefully apply a version of this mechanism.

Multiple Negative Partisanship and Bloc Parties

Emotional attachment to political parties is a dominant theme in electoral behavior research since the seminal analysis of American voting by a group of social psychologists in *The American Voter* (1960). Although this is typically seen as a singular attachment, this book has highlighted the usefulness of operationalizing the theory in a way that accommodates multiple attachments. This is especially useful in divided places in which party blocs operate (parties A, B, and so on representing community 1, and a different set of parties representing community 2). Furthermore, the overlooked aspect of negative attachment was emphasized and allied to multiple attachment in order to provide a theoretical handle on citizens' disengagement with the parties in "their" bloc. This notion of multiple negative attachments should be of use in other studies of consociational democracy.

Future Research

In addition to making suggestions about how other consociational democracies may be studied, I now focus again on the particular Northern Ireland case and outline suggested ways in which the research reported in this book could be valuably supplemented with further research.

Perhaps inevitably, the attempted answers provided in this book have prompted more questions—questions that will hopefully be addressed in future research, a number of which are now sketched.

Over-Time Analysis of Lower Preference Voting

The data used in this book were limited to first-preference vote and potential vote (likelihood of voting for a particular party). Comprehensive data on lower preference voting were not available for the 2007–2011 period examined. Assuming the collection of lower-preference data at the 2016 Assembly election, an over time comparison of lower-preference voting would be possible, comparing the first Assembly elections (1998 and 2003) to the 2016 election. This would provide high quality data with which to measure lower-preference cross-bloc voting, and change over time in the levels of such voting. This would provide evidence to assess the over time impact of consociational arrangements; has, as critics would suggest, cross bloc voting been constrained due to consociation's heightening of the ethnonational divide, or is there actually evidence of consociation coexisting with the lower-preference melting of the electoral blocs?

Northern Irish Identity

One particular type of citizen who may engage in cross-bloc lower preference voting are "Northern Irish" citizens. The meaning and political potency of the Northern Irish identity is certainly worthy of further investigation. What does this identity mean to its holder? Does the meaning vary across community? Does it credibly amount to an overarching, superordinate identity, with potential to act as a collective identity supplementing or replacing "Irish" and "British"? Or, for Catholics is it "Irish" by another name, and for Protestants simply another way of

manifesting a "British" identity? The evidence in this book suggests potential for "Northern Irish" to act as a "neutral" and overarching identity,
but qualitative investigation would aid interpretation here. The political
influence of Northern Irish identifiers has been examined in this book
and has been explicitly emphasized by a new (and short-lived) Northern
Ireland party—NI21—which sought to position itself as a moderate pro-
union party capturing the support of, in addition to Protestants, Catholics
who are not in favor of a united Ireland and any others who see themselves as "Northern Irish."

Emotions

In addition to the role of identity, moderate political behavior may
also be influenced by emotions. The role of distinct negative emotions in
driving political attitudes and behavior is increasingly being studied,
with particular emphasis on the distinction between anger and anxiety
(Huddy et al. 2007; Petersen 2010). Anxiety, perhaps counterintuitively, is
seen to be related to deliberation and evidence-based voting and reflec-
tion on the pros and cons of a particular political issue. In contrast, anger is based on habit-oriented behavior and the desire to identify guilty
parties and punish them. As Northern Ireland perhaps enters a phase of
significant political change with a decline in the importance of formerly
rigid distinctions, it is useful to consider the emotional drivers of such a
development. Specifically, one would expect that the predominant negative emotion of those for whom rigid ethnonational categories still operate would be anger, while the main negative emotion of those open to
moving away from habit-based attitudes and voting would be anxiety.
Imaginatively testing the proposition could cast light on the manner in
which emotion and reason—affect and cognition—interact in places over-
coming deep ethnonational division.

Appendix: Data

2007 Assembly Election Survey

The survey was conducted by Millward Brown Ulster (formerly Ulster Marketing Surveys). Forty-five randomly selected sampling points were used, and quota controls were used to ensure representation in terms of age, sex, class, socioeconomic position, and area. A quota sample of 1010 Northern Ireland citizens was interviewed face to face directly following the 7 March election. The survey captures extremely well the reality of voter behavior. Actual turnout at the election was 62.9 percent, and in the survey 61.6 percent of respondents reported that they had voted. In terms of reported vote choice, 7.5 percent of respondents indicated that they voted for the Alliance party (5.2 percent in the real election), 33.7 percent indicated that they voted for the DUP (30.1 percent in reality), 16.8 percent indicated that they voted UUP (14.9 percent in reality) 12.7 percent indicated that they voted for the SDLP (15.2 percent in reality), 22.8 percent indicated that they voted for Sinn Féin (26.2 percent in reality), and 7 percent indicated that they voted for another party or candidate (8 percent in reality).

2009 European Parliament Election Survey

A post-election telephone-based election study was conducted by Market Research Northern Ireland of 1013 respondents directly following the election, with sampling quotas set for age, sex, and social class. The post-election survey performs extremely well in capturing real world electoral behavior. The turnout rate in the 2009 European Parliament election in Northern Ireland was 42.8 percent (reported as 45.1 percent in the survey). In term of party choice, in the election 26.0 percent voted for Sinn Féin (24.9 percent in the survey), 18.2 percent voted for

Ulster Unionist Party (17.1 percent in the survey), 17.1 percent voted for the DUP (17.7 percent in the survey), 16.2 percent voted for the SDLP (15.8 percent in the survey), 13.7 percent voted for the TUV (12.9 percent in the survey), 5.5 percent voted for the Alliance (7.7 in the survey), 3.3 percent voted for the Green party (3.9 percent in the survey).

2010 Westminster Election Survey

A post-election quota-controlled telephone survey was conducted by Market Research Northern Ireland in the direct aftermath of the 2010 Westminster election ($N = 1,000$), with sampling quotas set for age, sex, and social class. The election survey represents very accurately citizens' actual vote choice in the 2010 election. The figures are (real world election result followed by survey estimate): Alliance (9.3, 6.3), DUP (25.8, 25.0), SDLP (15.8, 16.5), Sinn Féin (25.2, 25.5), UUP (14.8, 15.2), TUV (3.3, 3.9), others (5.8, 7.6). Turnout at the election was 57.6 percent, and the survey turnout estimate was 62.7 percent.

2011 Assembly Election Study

A post-election telephone survey (N=1200) was conducted by Market Research Northern Ireland (MRNI) with quotas set for age, gender, and religion within each of the 18 Electoral areas. Fieldwork was carried out between 18 May and 17 June 2011. The survey was co-funded by the Political Studies Association of Ireland (PSAI) and Queen's University Belfast. The election result (and survey estimate of that result) for each party is: DUP 30.0 (30.1), Sinn Féin 26.9 (26.1), UUP 13.2 (15.0), SDLP 14.2 (14.4), Alliance 7.7 (9.0), other 8.0 (5.4). Also, the turnout rate in the survey was 57.3 percent, very close to the reality of 55.7 percent.

Further Validation of the Surveys

Gschwendt (2005: 88) argues that in order to demonstrate the validity of using a quota-based sample (rather than a random selection-based sample), "scholars should gather as much external evidence as possible to argue that their achieved sample represents the population on as many dimensions as possible. The more evidence they are able to compile, the more confidence there is that their estimation results are robust even based on quota sample data." Distributions on ethnonational variables in these four surveys have very similar distributions to questions asked on the comparable annually conducted Northern Ireland Life and Times (NILT) survey based on random sampling (for example, questions relating to constitutional preferences and self-description as "unionist" "nationalist" or "neither unionist nor nationalist"): see Garry (2009, 2012, 2014a, b) for further discussion on this point. Overall, the surveys analyzed in this paper, while based on quota sampling, replicates well real world voting behavior and independently generated frequencies on important ethnonational issues derived from a random sampling-based survey.

Appendix Table A1: Logistic Regression Predicting Sinn Féin Rather Than SDLP Vote Choice

	log odds	SE	P
Ethnonational scale (0–6)	1.165	.114	.000
EU attitude scale (0–6)	.133	.111	.232
European Parliament election	−.966	.524	.065
EP election* EU attitude scale	.388	.199	.052
constant	−5.169	.646	.000
Nagelkerke r-square	.419		
n	438		

Pooled 2009 European Parliament and 2010 Westminster post-election surveys.

Appendix Table A2: Impact of Government Satisfaction on Vote Choice Conditional upon Attribution of Relative Influence of Parties in the Coalition

	Model 1			Model 2		
	DUP (rather than UUP)			(Sinn Féin rather than SDLP)		
	B	SE	P	B	SE	P
Satisfied with government (1 to 4)	0.092	0.271	0.735			
DUP more influential than UUP (scale)	−0.452	0.488	0.354			
Satisfied with government* DUP more influential than UUP (scale)	0.404	0.206	0.050			
(Ref=voted UUP 2007)						
Voted DUP in 2007	3.400	0.429	0.000			
Other 2007	2.054	0.393	0.000			
Satisfied with government (1 to 4)				0.452	0.317	0.155
SF more influential than SDLP (scale)				0.877	0.729	0.229
Satisfied with government* SF more influential than SDLP (scale)				−0.092	0.252	0.714
(Ref=voted SDLP 2007)						
Voted SF in 2007				1.585	0.379	0.000
Other 2007				1.114	0.353	0.002
unionist-nationalist (1–5 scale)	−.022	0.232	0.923	0.514	0.208	0.013
(ref=younger than 45)						
45 or older	0.180	0.331	0.586	−.587	0.321	0.072
(ref=C2DE)						
ABC1	−0.453	0.335	0.177	−0.208	0.327	0.525
Constant	−1.746	0.945	0.065	−3.654	1.254	0.004
N	277			245		
Nagelkerke r-square	.429			.255		

Appendix Table A3: Impact of Evaluations on Vote Choice Conditional upon Attribution of Responsibility

	DUP (rather than UUP)		
	B	SE	P
Protestants lives better (0 to 1 scale)	−3.018	1.008	0.003
DUP responsible	−4.491	1.259	0.000
Protestants lives better * DUP responsible	8.952	2.627	0.001
(ref = Voted UUP 2007)			
Voted DUP in 2007	3.507	0.447	0.000
Other 2007	2.090	0.384	0.000
unionist-nationalist (1–5 scale)	−0.023	0.218	0.917
(ref = younger than 45)			
45 or older	0.590	0.332	0.076
(ref = C2DE)			
ABC1	−0.249	0.322	0.440
Constant	0.194	0.714	0.785
N	291		
Nagelkerke r-square	.411		

Appendix Table A4: Binary Logistic Regressions Predicting Sinn Féin (Rather Than SDLP) Vote

	Model 1			Model 2			Model 3			Model 4		
	B	SE	P	B	SE	P	B	SE	P	B	SE	P
Catholic lives better (0 to 1 scale)	0.834	0.712	0.242									
Sinn Féin responsible	2.551	1.864	0.171									
Catholic lives better * SF responsible	−4.130	2.661	0.121									
Peace etc. better (0 to 1 scale)				0.283	0.587	0.630						
Sinn Féin responsible				−4.143	2.901	0.153						
Peace better * SF responsible				6.446	3.605	0.074						
Policing and justice better (0 to 1 scale)							0.033	0.627	0.958			
Sinn Féin responsible							0.164	0.459	0.722			
Policing better * SF responsible							−0.570	0.890	0.345			
Education better (0 to 1 scale)										0.871	0.642	0.175
Sinn Féin responsible										0.006	0.496	0.991

Education better * SF responsible										−0.015	1.247	0.990
(ref=Voted SDLP 2007)												
Voted Sinn Féin in 2007	1.882	0.376	0.000	1.811	0.375	0.000	1.840	0.371	0.000	2.070	0.402	0.000
Other 2007	1.262	0.336	0.000	1.381	0.331	0.000	1.302	0.329	0.000	1.414	0.352	0.000
unionist-nationalist (1–5 scale)	0.297	0.201	0.139	0.371	0.191	0.053	0.445	0.196	0.023	0.316	0.204	0.122
(ref=younger than 45)												
45 or older	−0.366	0.306	0.231	−0.477	0.300	0.112	−0.425	0.304	0.162	−0.289	0.314	0.357
(ref=C2DE)												
ABC1	−0.202	0.307	0.511	−0.172	0.303	0.571	−0.248	0.308	0.421	−0.039	0.317	0.902
Constant	−1.790	0.876	0.041	−1.850	0.852	0.030	−1.792	0.829	0.031	−1.941	0.822	0.018
N	261			273			268			243		
Nagelkerke r-square	.190			.225			.201			.231		

Appendix Table A5: Predicting Protestants' Propensity to Vote SDLP Rather Than Sinn Féin: OLS Regression

	co-eff.	se
(ref = female)		
Male	.165	.183
(ref = 45 plus)		
Younger than 45	.449*	.183
(ref = lower than degree)		
degree	.254	.225
(ref = c2de)		
abc1	.043	.188
(ref = British identity)		
Northern Irish identity	.134	.201
Unionist-nationalist scale (1–5)	.339**	.121
(ref = direct rule)		
pro-devolved administration	−.177	.191
pro-power sharing(1–5)	.077	.081
pro-tax and spend(1–3)	−.228	.141
pro-EU integration(1–5)	.081	.078
more positive evaluation of SDLP than Sinn Féin in terms of catch-all function	.552***	.046
Constant	.192	.505
N	455	
adjusted r-square	.28	

*.05 level, **.01 level, ***.001 level of statistical significance.

Appendix Table A6: Predicting Catholics' Propensity to Vote
UUP Rather Than DUP: OLS Regression

	co-eff.	se
(ref = female)		
Male	−.067	.238
(ref = 45 plus)		
Younger than 45	.222	.245
(ref = lower than degree)		
degree	−.174	.265
(ref = c2de)		
abc1	.363	.248
(ref = Irish identity)		
Northern Irish identity	.156	.298
Unionist-nationalist scale	−.094	.166
(ref = united Ireland)		
pro-devolved administration	−.230	.287
pro-power sharing(1–5)	−.101	.138
pro-tax and spend(1–3)	.287	.176
more positive evaluation of UUP than DUP in terms of catch-all function	.129	.077
Constant	.217	1.063
N	267	
adjusted r-square	.041	

*.05 level, **.01 level, ***.001 level of statistical significance.

Appendix Table A7: Binary logistic Regression Predicting Turnout at the 2011 Assembly Election

	Model 1 Protestants and Catholics			Model 2 Protestants and Catholics			Model 3 Protestants only			Model 4 Catholics only		
	B	SE	P	B	SE	P	B	SE	P	B	SE	P
(ref=abstained 2007)												
Voted 2007	1.498	0.182	0.000	1.500	0.182	0.000	1.396	0.262	0.000	1.296	0.305	0.000
Don't know/can't remember 2007	1.025	0.294	0.000	1.009	0.293	0.001	1.185	0.442	0.007	0.547	0.508	0.281
(ref=Protestants)												
Catholics	0.471	0.139	0.001	0.462	0.139	0.001						
NI govt responsible for issue areas (0-scale)	0.022	0.033	0.511									
Parties equally responsible on issue areas (0–7 scale)				0.006	0.044	0.887						
DUP/UUP have same influence on government							-0.116	0.181	0.520			
SF/SDLP have same influence on government										-0.266	0.238	0.260
constant	-0.225	0.150	0.135	-0.170	0.128	0.184	0.002	0.169	0.999	0.371	0.206	0.071
N	1006			1006			550			361		
Nagelkerke r-square	.109			.108			.075			.087		

Respondents of voting age at both elections included in the analysis.

Notes

Chapter 1. Consociation and Voting: Ideology, Performance, and Participation

1. The consociational approach is strongly associated with the writings of Lijphart (1969, 1975, 1977, 2004).

2. Paisley was replaced by Peter Robinson in 2008 as leader of the DUP and first minister.

3. Perhaps ironically, the relative merits of AV are one of the most contested aspects of academic debate on consociation (see discussion in Fraenkel and Grofman 2006a,b; Horowitz 2006).

4. The focus in this book is on the ability of *voters* to hold the executive to account. For a compelling examination of the extent to which *parliament* in Northern Ireland in the 2007–2011 period can hold the executive to account, see Conley (2012) and Conley and Dahan (2013).

5. Essentially, Downs-esque position undergirds Stokes-esque valence (Downs 1957; Stokes 1963; see Sanders et al. 2012).

Chapter 3. Ideology and Potential Support for British and Irish Parties

1. Speech in 2007 (http://www.labourpartyni.org/1114b).

2. This and subsequent quotes are taken from the report at http://sluggerotoole .com/2013/01/18/labour-ni-not-allowed-to-stand-candidates-an-abdication-of -responsible-political-leadership-at-a-time-when-we-have-a-leadership-void-in -ni/.

3. http://www.niconservatives.com/news/lord-feldman-spells-out-conservative -plans-northern-ireland.

Bibliography

Arceneaux, K. (2006). "The Federal Face of Voting: Are Elected Officials Held Accountable for the Functions Relevant to Their Office?" *Political Psychology* 27 (5): 731–45.

Anderson, C. (2000). "Economic Voting and Political Context: A Comparative Perspective." *Electoral Studies* 19 (2): 151–70.

——. (2006). "Economic Voting and Multilevel Governance: A Comparative Individual-Level Analysis." *American Journal of Political Science* 50 (2): 446–60.

Aughey, A. (1989). *Under Siege: Ulster Unionism and the Anglo-Irish Agreement.* Belfast: Blackstaff.

Brokington, D. (2004). "The Paradox of Proportional Representation: The Effect of Party Systems and Coalitions on Individuals' Electoral Participation." *Political Studies* 52 (3): 469–90.

Bogaards, M. and M. Crepaz. (2002) "Consociational Interpretations of the European Union" *European Union Politics* 3 (3): 357–81.

Brass, P. R. (1991). "Ethnic Conflict in Multiethnic Societies: The Consociational Solution and Its Critics." In P. Brass, ed., *Ethnicity and Nationalism: Theory and Comparison.* London: Sage. 333–48.

van der Brug, W., C. van der Eijk, and M. Franklin. (2007). *The Economy and the Vote: Economic Conditions and Elections in Fifteen Countries.* Cambridge: Cambridge University Press.

Budge, I. and D. Farlie. (1983). *Explaining and Predicting Elections: Issue Effects and Party Strategies in Twenty-Three Democracies.* London: Allen and Unwin.

Cairns, E. (2013) "Northern Ireland: Power Sharing, Contact, Identity, and Leadership." In J. McEvoy and B. O'Leary, eds., *Power Sharing in Deeply Divided Places.* Philadelphia: University of Pennsylvania Press.

Campbell, A., D. Converse, W. Miller, and D. Stokes. (1960). *The American Voter.* New York: Wiley.

Coakley, J. (2007). "National Identity in Northern Ireland: Stability or Change?" *Nations and Nationalism* 13 (4): 573–97.

———. (2008). "Ethnic Competition and the Logic of Party System Transformation." *European Journal of Political Research* 47: 766–93.

Conley, R. (2013). "Legislative Behaviour in the Northern Ireland Assembly, 2007–2011: Conflict and Consensus in a Developing Consociational Democracy." *Political Studies* 61: 179–97.

Conley, R. and C. Dahan (2012). "The Consociational Model and Question Time in the Northern Ireland Assembly: Policy Issues, Procedural Reforms, and Executive Accountability, 2007–2011." *Irish Political Studies* 37: 1–21.

Cutler, F. (2004). "Government Responsibility and Electoral Accountability in Federations." *Publius: The Journal of Federalism* 34 (2): 19–38.

———. (2008). "Whodunnit? Voters and Responsibility in Canadian Federalism." *Canadian Journal of Political Science* 41 (3): 627–54.

Downs, A. (1957). *An Economic Theory of Democracy.* New York: Harper and Row.

Duch, R. and R. Stevenson. (2008). *The Economic Vote: How Political and Economic Institutions Condition Election Results.* Cambridge: Cambridge University Press.

Duffy, M. and G. Evans. (1996). "Building Bridges? The Political Implications of Electoral Integration for Northern Ireland." *British Journal of Political Science* 26 (1): 123–40.

van der Eijk, C. (2002). "Design Issues in Electoral Research: Taking Care of (Core) Business." *Electoral Studies* 21: 189–206.

van der Eijk, C. and M. Franklin. (1996). *Choosing Europe? The European Electorate and National Politics in the Face of Union.* Ann Arbor: University of Michigan Press.

———. (2009). *Elections and Voters.* Basingstoke: Palgrave Macmillan.

van der Eijk, C. and C. Niemöller (1983). *Electoral Change in the Netherlands.* Amsterdam: CT Press.

Elliot, S. (2009). "The Electoral Dynamics of the Belfast Agreement." In B. Barton and P. Roche, eds., *The Northern Ireland Question: The Peace Process and the Belfast Agreement.* Basingstoke: Palgrave Macmillan.

Evans, E., and M. Duffy. (1997). "Beyond the Sectarian Divide: The Social Bases and Political Consequences of Nationalist and Unionist Party Competition in Northern Ireland." *British Journal of Political Science* 27: 47–81.

Evans, J., and J. Tonge. (2009). "Social Class and Party Choice in Northern Ireland's Ethnic Blocs." *West European Politics* 32: 1012–30.

Fiorina, M. (1981). *Retrospective Voting in American National Elections.* New Haven, Conn.: Yale University Press.

Fisher, S. and S. Hobolt. (2010). "Coalitions and Electoral Accountability." *Electoral Studies* 29 (3): 358–69.

Fraenkel, J. and B. Grofman. (2006a). "Does the Alternative Vote Foster Moderation in Ethnically Divided Societies? The Case of Fiji." *Comparative Political Studies* 39 (5): 623–51.

———. (2006b). "The Failure of the Alternative Vote as a Tool for Ethnic Moderation in Fiji: A Rejoinder to Horowitz." *Comparative Political Studies* 39 (5): 663–66.

Ganiel, G. (2009). " 'Battling in Brussels': The DUP and the European Union." *Irish Political Studies* 24 (4): 575–88.

Garry, J. (2007). "Making Party Identification More Versatile." *Electoral Studies* 26: 346–58.

———. (2009). "Consociationalism and Its Critics: Evidence from the Historic Northern Ireland Assembly Election of 2007." *Electoral Studies* 28: 458–66.

———. (2012). "Consociationalism, Regional Integration and Vote Choice: Northern Ireland and the 2009 European Parliament Election." *Acta Politica* 47: 113–27.

———. (2014a). "Potentially Voting Across the Divide in Deeply Divided Places: Ethnic Catch-All Voting in Consociational Northern Ireland." *Political Studies* 6 (S1): 2–19.

———. (2014b). "Holding *Parties* Responsible at Election Time: Multi-level, Multi-Party Government and Electoral Accountability." *Electoral Studies* 34: 78–88.

———. (2015). "How Context Shapes Individual Level Determinants of Political Participation: The Impact of Multiple Negative Party Identification on Turnout in Deeply Divided Northern Ireland." In M. Barrett and B. Zani, eds., *Political and Civic Engagement: Multidisciplinary Perspectives.* London: Routledge, 85–95.

Geys, B. (2006). "Explaining Voter Turnout: A Review of Aggregate Level Research." *Electoral Studies* 25 (4): 637–63.

Gilland-Lutz, K. and C. Farrington. (2006). "Alternative Ulster? Political Parties and the Non-Constitutional Policy Space in Northern Ireland." *Political Studies* 54: 715–42.

Gormley-Heenan, C. and R. MacGinty. (2008). "Ethnic Outbidding and Party Modernisation: Understanding the Democratic Unionist Party's Electoral Success in the Post-Agreement Environment." *Ethnopolitics* 7: 43–61.

Gschwendt, T. (2005). "Analysing Quota Sample Data and the Peer-Review Process." *French Politics* 3: 88–91.

Gudgin, G. (2009). "Implementing Devolved Government 1998–2002." In B. Barton and P. J. Roche, eds., *The Northern Ireland Question: The Peace Process and the Belfast Agreement*. Basingstoke: Macmillan, 57–83.

Hainsworth, P. and G. McCann. (2010). "Ringing Some Changes: The 2009 European Election in Northern Ireland." *Irish Political Studies* 25 (2): 303–14.

Hayes, B., I. McAllister, and L. Dowds. (2006) "In Search of the Middle Ground: Integrated Education and Northern Ireland Politics" ARK Research Update 42.

Henderson, A. and N. McEwan. (2010). "A Comparative Analysis of Voter Turnout in Regional Elections." *Electoral Studies* 23 (3): 405–16.

Hobolt, S. and J. Karp. (2010). "Voters and Coalition Governments." *Electoral Studies* 29 (3): 299–307.

Hobolt, S., J. Tilley, and S. Banducci. (2013). "Clarity of Responsibility: How Government Cohesion Conditions Performance Voting." *European Journal of Political Research* 52 (2): 64–187.

Hooghe, L. and G. Marks. (2001). *Multi-Level Governance and European Integration*. Lanham, Md.: Rowman & Littlefield.

Hooghe, L., G. Marks, and A. Schakel. (2010). *The Rise of Regional Authority: A Comparative Study of 42 Democracies (1950–2006)*. London: Routledge.

Horowitz, D. (1985). *Ethnic Groups in Conflict*. Berkeley: University of California Press.

———. (2001). "The Northern Ireland Agreement: Clear, Consociational and Risky." In J. McGarry, ed., *Northern Ireland and the Divided World: The Northern Ireland Conflict and the Comparative Perspective. Comparative Perspective*. Oxford: Oxford University Press.

———. (2002). "Africa: The Limits of Power-Sharing." *Journal of Democracy* 13: 123–36.

———. (2006). "Strategy Takes a Holiday: Fraenkel and Grofman on the Alternative Vote." *Comparative Political Studies* 39 (5): 652–62.

Huddy, L., S. Feldman, and E. Cassese (2007). "On the Distinct Political Effects of Anger and Anxiety." In R. Neumann et al., eds., *The Affect Effect: Dynamics of*

Emotion in Political Thinking and Behavior. Cambridge: Cambridge University Press. 202–30.

Johns, R. (2011). "Credit Where It's Due? Valence Politics, Attributions of Responsibility, and Multi-Level Elections." *Political Behavior* 33 (1): 53–77.

Jung, C. and I. Shapiro. (1995). "South Africa's Negotiated Transition: Democracy, Opposition, and the New Constitutional Order." *Politics & Society* 23 (3): 269–308.

Karp, J. and S. Banducci. (2008). "Political Efficacy and Participation in 27 Democracies: How Electoral Systems Shape Political Behaviour." *British Journal of Political Science* 38 (2): 311–34.

Keating, M. (2007). "Devolution and Public Policy Making." In P. Carmichael, C. Knox, and R. Osborne, eds., *Devolution and Constitutional Change in Northern Ireland.* Manchester: Manchester University Press. 231–42.

Key, V. O. (1966). *The Responsible Electorate.* New York: Vintage.

Kirchheimer, O. (1966). "The Transformation of the Western European Party Systems." In J. LaPalombara and M. Weiner, eds., *Political Parties and Political Development.* Princeton, N.J.: Princeton University Press.

Laver, M. and K. Shepsle, eds. (1994). *Cabinet Ministers and Parliamentary Government.* New York: Cambridge University Press.

———. (1998). *Making and Breaking Governments: Cabinets and Legislatures in Parliamentary Democracies.* New York: Cambridge University Press.

Lewis-Beck, M. (1990) *Economics and Elections: The Major Western Democracies.* Ann Arbor: University of Michigan Press.

Lijphart, A. (1969). "Consociational Democracy." *World Politics* 21: 207–25.

———. (1975). "The Northern Ireland Problem: Cases, Theories, and Solutions." *British Journal of Political Science* 5: 83–106.

———. (1977). *Democracy in Plural Societies: A Comparative Explanation.* New Haven, Conn.: Yale University Press.

———. (2004). "Constitutional Design for Divided Societies." *Journal of Democracy* 15: 98–109.

Maggiotto, M. and J. Pierson (1977). "Partisan Identification and Electoral Choice: The Hostility Hypothesis." *American Journal of Political Science*, 21: 745–67.

Maillot, A. (2009). "Sinn Féin's Approach to the EU: Still More 'Critical' Than 'Engaged'?" *Irish Political Studies* 24 (4): 559–74.

Marsh, M., R. Sinnott, J. Garry, and F. Kennedy. (2008). *The Irish Voter: The Nature of Electoral Competition in the Republic of Ireland*. Manchester: Manchester University Press.

Matthews, N. (2012). "The Northern Ireland Assembly Election, 2011." *Irish Political Studies* 27 (2): 341–58.

McCall, C. and L. O'Dowd. (2008). "Hanging Flower Baskets, Blowing in the Wind? Third Sector Groups, Cross-Border Partnerships and the EU Peace Programs in Ireland." *Nationalism and Ethnic Politics* 14 (1): 29–54.

McEvoy, J. (2006). "The Institutional Design of Executive Formation in Northern Ireland." *Regional and Federal Studies* 16 (4): 447–64.

———. (2007). "The Northern Ireland Assembly Election 2007." *Irish Political Studies* 22: 372–73.

McGarry, J. and B. O'Leary. (2009). "Power Shared After the Death of Thousands." In R. Taylor, ed., *Consociational Theory: McGarry/O'Leary and the Northern Ireland Conflict.*, London: Routledge. 15–84.

McKeown, S. (2014). "Perceptions of a Superordinate Identity in Northern Ireland." *Peace and Conflict: Journal of Peace Psychology* 20 (4): 505–15.

McLaughlin, P. (2009). "The SDLP and the Europeanization of the Northern Ireland Problem." *Irish Political Studies* 24 (4): 603–19.

Medeiros, M. and A. Noël. (2014). "The Forgotten Side of Partisanship: Negative Party Identification in Four Anglo-American Democracies." *Comparative Political Studies* 47 (7): 1022–46.

Mitchell, C. and J. Tilley. (2004). "The Moral Majority: Evangelical Protestants in Northern Ireland and Their Political Behaviour." *Political Studies* 52: 585–602.

Mitchell, P. and G. Evans. (2009). "Ethnic Party Competition and the Dynamics of Power Sharing in Northern Ireland." In R. Taylor, ed., *Consociational Theory: McGarry/O'Leary and the Northern Ireland Conflict*. London: Routledge. 146–64.

Mitchell, P., G. Evans, and B. O'Leary. (2009). "Extremist Outbidding in Ethnic Party Systems Is Not Inevitable: Tribune Parties in Northern Ireland." *Political Studies* 57: 379–421.

Morrow, D. and R. Wilson. (2007). "Political Parties and Elections." In R. Wilford and R. Wilson, eds., *Northern Ireland Devolution Monitoring Report—September 2007*. Report Prepared for Devolution Monitoring Programme 2006–8 of The Constitution Unit, University College London. 63–73.

Murphy, M. C. (2009). "Pragmatic Politics: The Ulster Unionist Party and the European Union." *Irish Political Studies* 24 (4): 589–602.

Noor, M., R. Brown, and G. Prentice. (2008) "Precursors and Mediators of Intergroup Reconcilitation in Northern Ireland: A New Model." *British Journal of Social Psychology* 47(3) 481–495.

Noor, M., R. Brown, L. Taggart, and A. Fernandez. (2010) "Intergroup Identity Perceptions and their Implications for Intergroup Forgivness: The Common Ingroup Identity Model and Its Efficacy in the Field." *Irish Journal of Psychology* 31 (3/4): 151–70.

O'Leary, B. (2005). "Debating Consociational Politics: Normative and Explanatory Arguments." In S. Noel, ed., *From Power Sharing to Democracy: Post-Conflict Institutions in Ethnically Divided Societies*. McGill-Queen's University Press.

———. (2013). "Power Sharing in Deeply Divided Places: An Advocate's Introduction." In J. McEvoy and B. O'Leary, eds., *Power Sharing in Deeply Divided Places*. Philadelphia: University of Pennsylvania Press.

O'Leary, B., B. Grofman, and J. Elklit (2005). "Divisor Methods for Sequential Portfolio Allocation in Multi-Party Executive Bodies: Evidence from Northern Ireland and Denmark." *American Journal of Political Science* 49 (1): 198–211.

Paldam, M. (1991). "How Robust is the Vote Function? A Study of Seventeen Nations over Two Decades." In H. Norpoth, M. Lewis-Beck, and J.-D. Lafay, eds., *Economics and Politics: The Calculus of Support*. Ann Arbor: University of Michigan Press. 9–32.

Petersen, M. B. (2010). "Distinct Emotions, Distinct Domains: Anger, Anxiety and Perceptions of Intentionality." *Journal of Politics* 72 (2): 357–65.

Petrocik, J. (1996). "Issue Ownership and Presidential Elections, with a 1980 Case Study." *American Journal of Political Science* 40 (3): 825–50.

Powell, B. and G. Whitten. (1993). "A Cross-National Analysis of Economic Voting: Taking Account of the Political Context." *American Journal of Political Science* 37 (2): 391–414.

Rabushka, A. and K. Shepsle. (1972). *Politics in Plural Societies: A Theory of Democratic Instability*. Columbus, Ohio: Merrill.

Reif, K. and H. Schmitt. (1980). "Nine Second-Order National Elections." *European Journal of Political Research* 8 (1): 3–44.

Richardson, B. (1991). "European Party Loyalties Revisited." *American Political Science Review* 85 (3): 751–75.

Roberts, H. (1990). "Sound Stupidity: The British Party System and the Northern Ireland Question." In J. McGarry and B. O'Leary, eds., *The Future of Northern Ireland*. Oxford: Clarendon.

Sanders, D., H. D. Clarke, M. C. Stewart, and P. Whiteley. (2012). "Downs, Stokes and the Dynamics of Electoral Choice." *British Journal of Political Science* 41: 287–314.

Schmitt, H. (2002). "Multiple Party Identifications." Paper prepared for Conference of the Comparative Study of Electoral Systems (CSES) at the WZB in Berlin, 21–24 February.

Stokes, D. (1963). "Spatial Models of Party Competition." *American Political Science Review* 57 (2): 368–77.

Tannam, E. (2010). "Northern Ireland and the EU: Europeanisation and Hibernicisation?" In C. McCall and T. Wilson, eds., *Europeanisation and Hibernicisation: Ireland and Europe*. Amsterdam: Rodopi.

Tilley, J. and G. Evans (2011). "Political Generations in Northern Ireland." *European Journal of Political Research* 50 (5): 583–608.

Tilley, J., G. Evans, and C. Mitchell. (2008). "Consociationalism and the Evolution of Political Cleavages in Northern Ireland, 1989–2004." *British Journal of Political Science*, 38 (4): 699–717.

Weisberg, H. (1999). "Political Partisanship." In J. Robinson, P. Shaver, and L. Wrightsman, eds., *Measures of Political Attitudes*. San Diego: Academic Press. 681–729.

Whitten, G. and H. Palmer. (1999). "Cross-National Analyses of Economic Voting." *Electoral Studies* 18 (1): 49–67.

Wilford, R. (2010). "The Politics of Constraint." *Parliamentary Affairs* 63 (1): 134–55.

Wolinetz, S. (2002). "Beyond the Catch-All Party: Approaches to the Study of Parties and Party Organization in Contemporary Democracies." In J. Linz, J. Montero, and R. Gunther, eds., *The Future of Political Parties*. Oxford: Oxford University Press. 136–65.

Index

Acknowledgments

I would like to thank the British Academy for very generously funding my position as British Academy Mid-Career Research Fellow 2012–2013. The twelve-month research leave facilitated my writing of this book. The Political Studies Association of Ireland (PSAI) very generously contributed to the funding of the 2011 post-election survey. Any royalties for this book will be given to the PSAI in partial recompense for their contribution. Josie Knowles and Neil Matthews read and commented on the final draft of the book, which is very much appreciated, and Brendan O'Leary was very generously supportive and enthusiastic about the manuscript. I would also like to thank the 4,223 Northern Ireland citizens who, for no recompense, very generously gave their time to answering the four post-election surveys on which this book is based. Their cooperation is sincerely appreciated.

Chapter 4 draws upon work I previously published as "Holding *Parties* Responsible at Election Time: Multi-Level, Multi-Party Government and Electoral Accountability," *Electoral Studies* 34 (2014): 78–88 and Chapter 5 draws upon work I previously published as "Potentially Voting Across the Divide in Deeply Divided Places: Ethnic Catch-All Voting in Consociational Northern Ireland, *Political Studies* 62 (S1) (2014): 2–19. I am grateful to Elsevier and Wiley respectively).

Finally, and especially, I would like to thank Arthur, Daniel, and Maria.